cc

Items should be returned on or before the last date
shown below. Items not already requested by other
borrowers may be renewed in person, in writing or by
telephone. To renew, please quote the number on the
barcode label. To renew online a PIN is required.
This can be requested at your local library.
Renew online @ **www.dublincitypubliclibraries.ie**
Fines charged for overdue items will include postage
incurred in recovery. Damage to or loss of items will
be charged to the borrower.

Leabharlanna Poiblí Chathair Bhaile Átha Cliath
Dublin City Public Libraries

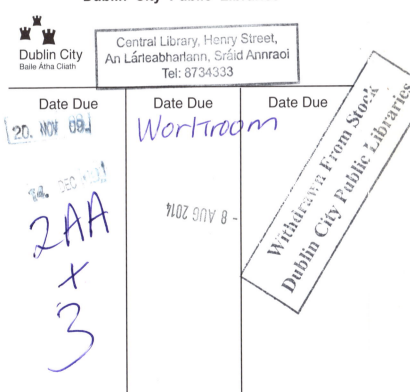

Dublin City
Baile Átha Cliath

Central Library, Henry Street,
An Lárleabharlann, Sráid Annraoi
Tel: 8734333

Date Due	Date Due	Date Due
20. NOV 09	Workroom	
DEC	- 8 AUG 2014	
2AA		
x		
3		

ALSO BY JOAN McBREEN

POETRY
The Wind Beyond the Wall
Story Line Press, Oregon, 1990, reprinted 1991.

A Walled Garden in Moylough
Story Line Press, Oregon and Salmon Poetry, Co. Clare, 1995.

Winter in the Eye - New and Selected Poems
Salmon Poetry, Co. Clare, 2003.

Heather Island
Salmon Poetry, Co. Clare, 2009.

AS EDITOR
The White Page – An Bhileog Bhán: Twentieth-Century Irish Women Poets
Salmon Poetry, Co. Clare, 1999, reprinted 2000, 2001, 2007 (anthology).

CD
The Long Light on the Land – Selected Poems: read to a background of traditional Irish airs and classical music
Ernest Lyons Productions, Cloondeash, Castlebar, Co. Mayo, 2004.

The Watchful Heart

A New Generation of Irish Poets

Poems and Essays

EDITED AND PRESENTED BY

JOAN McBREEN

salmonpoetry

Published in 2009 by
Salmon Poetry
Cliffs of Moher, County Clare, Ireland
Website: www.salmonpoetry.com
Email: info@salmonpoetry.com

ISBN 978-1-907056-03-1 Paperback
ISBN 978-1-907056-04-8 Hardback

Cover artwork: Kevin Cosgrove's *Big Digger* (2007), The Deering Delany Collection.
Courtesy of the artist and Mother's Tankstation, Contemporary Art Gallery, Dublin.

Typesetting & Design: Siobhán Hutson

for Niall MacMonagle
with gratitude

Contents

Guest Preface

'A box where sweets compacted lie' is how the seventeenth-century poet George Herbert described the season of spring, but the phrase equally well fits this anthology. Apart from her own work as a poet, as editor Joan McBreen has already done a conspicuous service to Irish letters in her 1999 Salmon anthology of twentieth-century women poets, *The White Page / An Bhileog Bhán*, since reprinted three times. *The Watchful Heart* also merits a warm welcome. Representing poets of both genders, all aged fifty or under, it is conceived more spaciously, offering three poems apiece by twenty-four poets, plus a short essay by each. Well-planned and carefully assembled, it adds to the pleasures of all good collections a distinctive bonus: as readers we get to hear each poet's voice in, so to speak, two mediums: poetry and reflective prose.

It gives a fascinating cross-section of Irish poetry at the present time. All the contributing poets are accomplished, having published two or more collections. They include ten women and fourteen men, one poet in Irish, a couple working bilingually, the rest in English; poets resident in Ireland and elsewhere, poets north and south and – perhaps more unusually – east and west. Some have achieved wider dissemination or more prestigious publication than others. In terms of style and language some show strong formalist credentials, achieving stylish, funny, often moving pieces (Alan Gillis, Justin Quinn, Margaret Galvin's fine 'Service', whose unobtrusive pentameter perfectly expresses its theme) others show force and eloquence while working with looser, though by no means disorderly, forms (Louis de Paor, Peter Sirr, Mary O'Donoghue). Several push the bounds of conventional lyric technique, experimenting with longer lines. Paul Perry's powerful poem about the abandoned Roanoke colony, and Damian Smyth's fine work, are well worth knowing. There are agreeable contrasts here, in a landscape constantly shifting and re-forming as you read or browse. The essays are a pleasurable narrative in themselves: while wearing their intelligence lightly they offer insights from many angles into the practices of poetry and its many modes of existence. Leontia Flynn is wryly funny about the felt compulsion to write. Louis de Paor develops a witty, perceptive meditation on the processes of translation. David Wheatley, on the superficially unpromising topic of Hull's industrialised riverside, suggests that "maybe the places we love become blind spots to us in the end, migrating inwards to chosen versions of themselves in our mind's eye, as Ireland has become for me, these days".

The collection has an unusual range, thanks to Joan McBreen's inspired drawing together of several faces of Irish poetry now. More academic, professionalised poets are cheek by jowl with other kinds. Kevin Higgins offers sassy, stylish oral poetry and a spirited justification of the continuing orality of Irish culture, as registered in the "open microphone" culture of several cities and in thriving workshops far and wide (each a vital poets' nursery in twenty-first century Ireland, particularly for women poets, as several essays note). There is Gearóid Mac Lochlainn's passionate bilingual and trans-national narrative work, and Kate Newmann's riveting patchwork essay, compounded of teenage workshop work on dark themes, itself caught in the act of becoming poetry, like Wheatley's. Cherry Smyth's fine poems are matched by a sharp, intelligent essay reframing some of those fundamental questions about speech and silence which good poetry should always raise. Like McBreen's quietly enabling work on the whole book, this piece wears its discernment lightly. It does not pronounce on ideologies or factions, but – as Smyth says of poetry – "allows silence and speech, flesh and spirit, time and its transcendence, to cross over the threshold and back", in whichever mode each poet chooses.

Patricia Coughlan
April 2009

Patricia Coughlan is a Professor at the School of English, University College, Cork.

Editor's Introduction

'The lines flow from the hand unbidden
and the hidden source is the watchful heart.'

from *Everything Is Going To Be All Right*
– Derek Mahon

This anthology aims to be a guide and a stimulating companion to readers of Irish poetry everywhere. It presents the work, both poems and essays, of twenty-four Irish poets born in the last fifty years.

Since compiling and editing *The White Page - An Bhileog Bhán: Twentieth-Century Irish Women Poets*, I frequently thought about working on a similar volume of younger poets. Lovers of poetry and of Irish poetry everywhere like to buy anthologies.

In early 2008 I decided to go ahead with work on *The Watchful Heart – A New Generation of Irish Poets – Poems and Essays*. I then had to decide what my criteria for inclusion in this new book would be.

I invited contributions from poets who had published at least two collections of poetry. Because twenty-two female poets who fitted the age profile and other criteria had already been included in *The White Page* (in its third reprint as I write), it was decided not to include them. To do so would have made the book a far larger one than I, or Salmon Poetry, had in mind.

I sent out a general letter of invitation to many younger Irish poets, male and female. I asked them to contribute three poems which had not previously been published in collections but which could have appeared in journals or newspapers, been broadcast or anthologised. I also asked for a short essay focusing on poetry, the writing of poetry or any aspect of it that was of personal interest to them. The response, overall, was immediately enthusiastic and generous.

In agreement with my publisher, Jessie Lendennie, I set out

to represent some of what I felt would be the best of recent Irish poetry but would not necessarily be comprehensive or all-inclusive.

As I began to compile and read the poets' material, I realised that they were indeed in the process of making their way, bravely taking chances and experimenting in their work.

This work will appeal to different readers; some will appeal across generations, more will stimulate and excite younger readers. The inclusion of short biographies, bibliographies and photographs will, I hope, be of special interest to international readers of Irish poetry and literature.

Ireland has always had a lively interaction with her writers, especially her poets. The last two decades and more have seen a great many poetry readings, literary festivals, poetry workshops, radio and television interviews and feature programmes with writers and poets.

The names, work and faces of many of the poets in this anthology will be familiar to readers, some more than others. It is also interesting to me as editor to be made aware of the many different hats the included poets wear. Careers in universities, publishing, arts administration and broadcasting are noted. A remarkable number have been honoured with prestigious literary prizes, nationally and internationally. In an introduction such as this, I am reluctant to single out individual poets for special mention. Better to allow readers form their own opinion of the work, to make their own choices with regard to the poems they will be attracted to, find exciting, fresh and revealing.

There is a sense of a European rather than a national sensibility in the air around much of the work. Humour features, too, and is not striving for effect. That poets contributed essays or short prose pieces will, I hope, be a source of added interest. Readers like to know something of the background of poets, the places where the poet lives and works, who his or her influences are. All of this is reflected in this anthology. As editor, I thank the contributors for sharing so much of themselves in this regard.

As stated, the twenty-four poets featured do not represent a complete picture of the poetic scene in Ireland today. They can, however, be taken as representative of the broad range of poetry being written and published in the recent past and at present. It is a range that reflects variety, technical competence and attention to the world. Of course there are many other fine young Irish poetic voices. Their omission will irritate, puzzle or frustrate some readers. But any anthology has to make choices: the editor's difficult task consists of excluding as well as including.

One way or another these twenty-four voices should be heard as part of a conversation, in a long and often vexed tradition, in Irish poetry as in politics. Ultimately, like all serious, thoughtful poets writing against the silences of their time and location, they strive to make our world intelligible.

The Irish poet Louis MacNeice sums something like this up in his 1937 poem *The Brandy Glass*

> Only let it form within his hands once more –
> The moment cradled like a brandy glass.
> Sitting alone in the empty dining hall....
> From the chandeliers the snow begins to fall
> Piling around the carafes and table legs
> And chokes the passage of the revolving door.
> The last diner, like a ventriloquist's doll
> Left by his master, gazes before him, begs:
> 'Only let it form within my hands once more.'

Joan McBreen
April 2009

Poems and Essays

Poems and Essays

Pat Boran
(1963-)

Born and grew up in Portlaoise, Co Laois. Now living in Dublin. He won the Patrick Kavanagh Award in 1989 and has published four collections of poetry. Selected volumes of his poetry have appeared in Italian, Hungarian and Macedonian editions. His fiction publications include *Strange Bedfellows* (Salmon, 1991) and the children's title *All the Way from China* (1999), shortlisted for the Bisto Book of the Year Award. His non-fiction includes *The Portable Creative Writing Workshop* (1999/2005). *Wingspan – A Dedalus Sampler*, an anthology of Dedalus poets, was edited by Pat Boran and published by the press in 2006. For many years he was programme director of the Dublin Writers' Festival, and held residencies with Dublin City Libraries, Dublin Corporation and Dublin City University. He has presented The Poetry Programme on RTÉ Radio 1 and the books programme Undercover on RTÉ television. He is currently editor of The Dedalus Press. In 2007 he became a member of Aosdána. In 2008 he received the Lawrence O'Shaughnessy Award for Poetry.

POETRY COLLECTIONS

The Unwound Clock. (1990). Dublin, The Dedalus Press.
Familiar Things. (1993). Dublin, The Dedalus Press.
The Shape of Water. (1996). Dublin, The Dedalus Press.
As the Hand, the Glove. (2001). Dublin, The Dedalus Press.

Dream of the Sparrow Morning

Dream of the Sparrow Morning:
a line from some imagined Chinese poem,

or a fragment of wisdom,
blurred by translation,

or something glanced at, flicked through
in a bookshop somewhere
years ago,

and forgotten
until now,

the line Dream of the Sparrow Morning
comes back to you,
comes back *for* you,

wakes just before you do
in the dawn light,
to whisper in your ear.

And the more you think on it,
puzzle over it,
the more the phrase
professes no great
interest in meaning.

Dream of the Sparrow Morning:
five words finding each other,
like a burst of colour on a hillside field,
the wild flowers of language.

And yet, now, watch as they lend themselves,
title-like, to everything you see:

your shirt and jeans draped over the chair,
your shoes standing by to useless attention,
your curled up wristwatch on the bedside-table,
foetal, like you; and, like you, blank in the early light.

Dream of the Sparrow: Morning.

Dream of the Sparrow-Morning.

Or, my favourite interpretation,
Dream of the Sparrow (comma) Morning.
An exhortation. A prayer of breath.
A call for this bright morning to produce
that plump brown-grey short-tailed bird
whom Sappho imagined
drawing Aphrodite's chariot
through the heavens.

Dream of the Sparrow, Morning.
The soft landing of that comma
between Sparrow and Morning
perfect somehow,
(the happy accident of its worm-like appearance)
as you draw back the curtains to reveal
the lawn outside and find
the sparrows have indeed arrived
before you, have settled, all business,
dreamt up by morning, conjured by it,
and making the most of the light.

Let's Die

'Let's die,' I say to my kids,
Lee aged five, Luca not yet three,
and under an August blanket of sun
we stretch out in the grass on a hill
to listen to the sea just below
drawing close, pulling back,
or the sheep all around us
crunching their way down towards earth.

'Do you love the clouds, Dada?'
'Do you love the Pink Panther?'
and 'Will you stay with us for ever?'
to which I reply, without hesitation,
Yes, Yes and Yes again,
knowing that as long as we lie here
everything is possible, that any of the paths
up ahead might lead anywhere
but still, just in time, back home.

Like me, sometimes they act too much,
fill the available space and time
with fuss and noise and argument,
but up here, overlooking the landscape,
the seascape, of their lives, on this hill
they like to play this game, to lie
together and together to die
which, in their children's language, means
less to expire or to cease
than to switch to Super Attention Mode,
to prepare for travel, to strap oneself
into the booster seat and wait and wait
for the gradual but inexorable lift
off and up and out into motion.

Mary Branley
(1962-)

Born and grew up in Sligo. She left Ireland in the 1980s for the U.S.A. and the U.K. She worked as a primary and secondary teacher, completing her M.Ed. in Boston in Intercultural Studies in 1992. Since 2001 she has worked with Kids' Own Publishing Partnership, a non-profit arts organisation that promotes children as writers and artists, and with the publication of thirteen books, written and illustrated by children. Her poetry has appeared in *Europe is a Woman*, (ed. Anna Aguilar Amat, Autonomous University of Barcelona) and in *Barcelona 2007* an anthology of European women's poetry with Catalan translations.

POETRY COLLECTIONS

A Foot on the Tide. (2002). Donegal, Summer Palace Press.
Martin Let Me Go. (2009). Donegal, Summer Palace Press.

Spent

How is it
with this love that

one moment, I shout in joy
the next I cry in anguish

as each door opens?
Though you approach in gentleness,

I thrash like a baby that
will not settle in your arms,

wailing, as
the ocean mourns.

The universe in her wisdom
holds the ocean in.

All this grief because I love you?
My heart is sore and unused to love.

All this love, because the grief is spent.
Your heart has emptied out;

a coastal cave at low tide
where you and I find rest.

Sé do bheatha a Mhuire

There was something
in the way they said the rosary,

rhythmic reach and pull
as if we were sitting in a currach

skimming the waves.
Sé do bheatha a Mhuire

lift and drop
atá lán de ghrásta

rattle and whist
of the *máidí raimhe*

Tá an Tiarna leat
arms outstretched

in a perfect arc
is beannaithe thú idir mná

the pull to the heart
and over lap *na peacaigh anois*

and at the sacred hour
tabhair dom do lámha

row me across to Inis Meáin
ar dhuirling bán,

row with all your love
to bring me *slán abhaile.*

NOTES

Sé do bheatha a Mhuire: Hail Mary
atá lán de ghrásta: full of grace
máidí raimhe: oars
Tá an Tiarna leat: the Lord is with thee
beannaithe thú idir mná: blesséd art thou amongst women
na peacaigh anois: our sins now
tabhair dom do lámha: give me your hands
ar dhuirling bán: on a white beach
slán abhaile: safely home

Ruth

The first mother you chose
hid you in her womb
for as long as she could.
You have her eyes,
her smile, her sorrow.

She held you for a week
before she took you
to the lily pond knowing
that kindness would find you
Panzi Wu.

The second mother
dreamt of you for years,
before she set out
on the long journey
to the lily pond.

She will ignite
your smile. She will
take your mother's sorrow
and remember.
She will call you Ruth.

NOTE

Panzi Wu means abandoned by the lily pond.
Ruth is Hebrew for sorrow.

15

Leland Bardwell

Poet, playwright, novelist and short story writer, Leland Bardwell has been a unique voice in the Irish literary world for over sixty years. Her passion for life, love, language and writing has brought her readers into unusual terrain. Her sense of being an outsider from a Protestant background in Catholic Ireland, a maverick in literary and feminist circles, informs her poetry and novels. The worst does happen to Bardwell's characters, abuse and abandonment, betrayal in relationships, failure and addiction, yet all are saved somewhat by humour and compassion. Leland, as a co-editor of *Cyphers*, a poetry magazine in publication for over thirty years, and co-founder of the Irish Writers' Co-Op in Dublin in the 1980s, has helped many writers start their careers. Scriobh, a literary festival she established in Sligo in 1993 with writers Molly McCloskey and Jean Valentine, combined her love for literature with her legendary hospitality and love of parties. But behind these achievements and contributions to Irish contemporary writing, Leland is humble, self-deprecating and shy beyond belief.

In her long life, she has lived in Birmingham, London, Paris, and many different parts of Ireland. Though her early life was spent in India and Leixlip, County Kildare, she now resides in Cloonagh, North Sligo, 'exposed on the cliffs of the heart' (Rilke), as near the sea as you can possibly get. Her door is always open to fellow-poets, visitors and stray cats. Over the past ten years, Leland and

I have become dear friends. We have shared many a glass of wine, a few trips together, trials and tribulations. As a mentor, critic and editor, Leland has been unstinting in her support for my work and for that I am deeply grateful.

Leland Bardwell is more widely read, known and loved than she would like to admit, but a small episode illustrates this point. When the Model Niland Art Gallery was opened officially in 2001, we were there with a throng of Sligo people to celebrate the occasion. Our cheerful and gracious President, Mary McAleese was invited to help celebrate the local and national vision of having such a flagship gallery outside Dublin.

The high-ceilinged atrium is usually cool and airy, but on this day the heat, the humidity and press of people kept us far back, close to the main doors. It wasn't a bad position, near the wine, or the outside, when we needed to go for a smoke. We all smoked in those days. We listened intently to the President congratulate local efforts on the ground, going back to the days of Nora Niland. Ms. Niland, an inspired County Librarian, was responsible for collecting numerous paintings of Jack B.Yeats and others, and was one of the founders of the International Yeats Summer School. Now her collection had a state-of-the-art permanent home. We were proud.

After her speech, our President was brought on a tour of the galleries. We went outside to mingle and chat. Half an hour later, we noticed the State Mercedes at the bottom of the steps. The President was leaving shortly. We waited for her to come out. She emerged all smiles and handshakes and out of the corner of her eye, spotted a familiar face.

'Leland,' she exclaimed in delight, extending her hand.

'Mary', said Leland equally delighted.

'Leland and I go back a long way,' the President explained. 'We were both in the same Irish class, a long time ago. And Leland was the teacher's pet.'

Leland giggled. 'You were very good too.'

'It's great to see you', the President said, being ushered to the waiting car and off to her next appearance.

'What Irish class?' I asked Leland later. She and Mary McAleese spent weeks attending an Irish intensive course run by Conradh na Gaeilge in the 1980s.

A Restless Life, Leland's memoir, was published in 2008 by Liberties Press. It gives a fascinating account of her life to the end of the 1960s and the end of an era in literary Dublin. Much to her surprise, it has been widely praised as a magnificent read, with more than one reviewer calling for a movie of the book to be made. But it would provide some challenge for an actress to portray the nine lives of a woman constantly re-inventing herself in response to tumultuous times.

Though she dedicated the memoir to her parents, Mary and Pat Hone, Leland is unflinching in describing her childhood as the unloved youngest of three. The first half of the memoir is peppered with her father's love letters to her mother, from the trenches of World War I, not in the British army but a division of the Second Canadian Signallers. Like thousands of Irish men fighting the Germans, he had strong Sinn Féin loyalties when the 1916 Rising took place.

At odds with her family, Leland wandered the fields, rivers Rye and Liffey and the woods round Leixlip, Co Kildare alone. I have always envied Leland's freedom from formal schooling in her childhood. She did go to Alexandra College, Dublin when she was twelve years old. Though very bright, Leland was not encouraged to go on to third level. Instead she and her sister were carers for their mother, dying slowly and painfully from cancer. Her life changed irrevocably when she became pregnant and fled to Birmingham to have the baby, leaving her old life behind forever at twenty-one. From then on she lived on the edge, in a turmoil that often made her reckless. Through lost loves, challenging relationships and numerous disappointments, Leland faced all with uncommon resilience, and without an iota of self-pity. Friends and friendship sustained her, and still do.

Leland may have to reconsider her position as outsider, as her words and her life have earned her respect across the board. If she hasn't already read Leland's memoir, I'm sure it's on our President's list.

Patrick Chapman
(1968-)

 Born in Roscommon and grew up in Boyle. He is a poet, fiction-writer and screenwriter. Together with four poetry collections, he has written a collection of stories *The Wow Signal* (Bluechrome 2007) and *Burning the Bed* (2003), a multi-award-winning film starring Gina McKee and Aidan Gillen. He also wrote an audio play *Doctor Who: Fear of the Daleks* (Big Finish 2007). He won first prize for a story in the 2003 *Cinescape* Genre Literary Awards in Los Angeles. In 2001 he collaborated with Gemma Tipton on the Foot Series art exhibitions. In 2006 he co-founded the Irish Literary Revival website with Philip Casey. Patrick Chapman was a finalist in the *Sunday Tribune*/Hennessy Awards for poetry in 1995 and for fiction in 1999.

POETRY COLLECTIONS

Jazztown. (1991). Dublin, Raven Arts Press.
The New Pornography. (1996). Co. Clare, Salmon Poetry.
Breaking Hearts and Traffic Lights. (2007). Co. Clare, Salmon Poetry.
A Shopping Mall on Mars. (2008). New York, BlazeVOX Books.

The Darwin Vampires

Being loth to sink in at your neck, they prefer to drink
Between your toes. They revel in the feet; they especially
Enjoy those places in between, where microbial kingdoms,
Overthrown with a pessary, render needle-toothed
Injuries invisible; where any trace of ingress, lost in the fold,

Is conspicuous – as they themselves in daylight are –
By its absence. You will hardly notice that small
Sting; might not miss a drop until the moment
That the very last is drained. And when you're six
Beneath the topsoil, you will never rise to join them.

Rather, you will be a hint; a fluctuating butterfly;
A taste-regret on someone's tongue; a sudden tinted
Droplet in the iris of a fading smile; a blush upon
A woman's rose; a broken vein in someone's eyelid;
Always one degree below what's needed to be warm.

Love Watches For Death

1

Love watches for Death. She watches the road.
She waits for her Death to come home.

When he does, he is mute. He must keep his own counsel
Regarding his time in the desert

In order that he does not burden her conscience
With knowledge of deeds he has done in her name.

2

Love watches for Death. She waits for her stud
To come home to their bed, for she misses his touch;

She's deprived of the heat of a body that's rightfully hers;
And wasn't she promised the comfort and strength of a man?

3

Love watches for Death. When her Death returns home
He says nothing to Love of the children he's maimed;

Of the men he has burned so a town could be saved.
If he tells her the truth of it though he can barely

Believe it himself, she'll disown him as some sort of
Changeling. When Death

Gives not even a word;
When he fails to expose the old stain on his heart

So that she can consider her own unbesmirched,
Love denounces his silence.

And Death –
Without a defence against Love's disappointment –

Takes to the desert again,
In search of a quantum of peace.

Gloria Mundi

In that recurring future memory
I push out from the capsule's
Open hatch – my Mercury
Recalling Alan Shepard's.
Snug within a pressure suit,
I'm paid out on the tether line
That tautens until,
Breaking tensile limits, it whips free,
Unleashing an infinity
In which I feel no terror.
Rather, lost in wonder at the sky,
I find a liberation in accepting
That I'll die out here.
There's nowhere I would rather die.
Moreover, beatifically
Mislaid between the moon
And Cape Canaveral,
I revel in being utterly alone,
Elated in my weightlessness;
The last breath in my lungs expelled
To hush a fragile wisp
From that frail atmosphere
Of bygone Earth above where
Nature ever dared to blow.
The flower of an astral ghost,
My final inhalation, leaves
A shrinking mist upon the glass.
Embalmed by space and gliding
Out of orbit, now descending
To cremation-by-re-entry –
I desire within my reverie
To settle on the solar wind,
And float serenely far beyond Centauri.

Fortune Cookies

When you write from the heart, there will be blood.

You'll be surprised at how much trouble a really good love poem can get you into.

It's OK to make the Grecian Urn all over again, as long as you have something to put in it.

People seem to think that poetry is Truth when it is in fact as artificial as a glass star designed to refract Beauty.

If you got into writing poems because you thought they took less time than stories, you were misinformed.

With all that is going on in the world, it is increasingly difficult to write for posterity.

A poem is sometimes a photograph made of words rather than light.

It doesn't do to discourage those who write badly now; who knows what wonderful poems they will write in the future.

If an idea has potential, it will pester you in your dreams; but a poem shouldn't be written until it's ready to come out.

Procrastination is your friend.

Nature can be inspiring because it doesn't care about you, so it is not putting on an act.

Concrete and steel are as important as nature. Plastic is good.

The human condition is interesting as a subject but it helps to be more specific.

If the pram in the hall is really the enemy of promise, steal the time you need to write, even if it makes you unpopular with your partner.

Your ancestors will not be proud of your work, because they are dead.

Poetry itself is rarely an interesting subject for a poem.

Writing workshops can yield good poems, but not until long afterwards.

It is all very well to be the voice of a generation, but it is unlikely that the generation in question is saying anything that requires your voice with which to say it.

It is not easy to describe a tornado well while it is tossing you about.

Poetry equals turbulence plus time.

Unlike a song, a poem must contain all of its music within the words.

Death is always a good subject for poetry. The poet's own death is a great subject for poetry. If a poem about his own death is written posthumously by the poet, that is a remarkable poem.

A good teacher can show you the way but it is you who must walk it.

Schools of poetry are like schools of fish.

It is not true that poetry changes nothing; before the poem was written, it did not exist.

The epic poem has been replaced by the blockbuster movie. *Jaws* is the new *Beowulf*.

Robert Lowell was on to something when he wrote 'To Speak of Woe That Is in Marriage'.

When you sit down to make a poem, tell yourself that nobody will ever read it. This frees you to write whatever comes out, without inhibition or self-censorship.

The second draft is when you get to protect your sources.

Poetry is good at bearing witness but technology is better.

Oral history means something different these days.

If you're a poet, you're always writing, even if you're staring into space, or in love. This can be disconcerting for those around you.

The poet used to be the conscience of a community, back when communities had consciences.

Civilians do not understand.

As William Goldman observed about the movies, one could also say about poetry: nobody knows anything.

Poetry as an art-form cannot be taught; it can only be transmitted, like smallpox.

Well-made religious poetry is either beautiful in its artifice or heartbreaking in its implications: a glorious monument to a vast, empty sky.

Criticism is important but bad reviews are always too late to be useful.

Live as much as possible in the now, whenever that is.

Inspiration can come from anywhere; it's where it goes that counts.

Visible light is only a minuscule fraction of all the wavelengths there are in the electromagnetic spectrum; try seeing with some of those others when writing a poem.

If there's one thing a poem can't do, it's write itself.

Work is where poetry's heart begins to beat. In the final poem, that work must be invisible.

Deadlines are inspiring. Use as many as necessary, as often as necessary.

To write poetry, it helps if you are a little weird.

The other art form that poetry most closely resembles is sculpture.

A rainbow is a poem, according to the sky. Mind your head.

Louis de Paor
(1961-)

Born and grew up in Cork. Louis de Paor has been involved with the contemporary renaissance of poetry in Irish since 1980. He was first published in the poetry journal *Innti* which he subsequently edited for a time. A four times winner of the Seán Ó Ríordáin/Oireachtas Award, the premier award for a new collection of poems in Irish, he lived in Australia from 1987 to 1996. His first bilingual collection *Aimsir Bhreicneach/ Freckled Weather* was shortlisted for the Victorian Premier's Award for Literary Translation. He was also granted a Writer's Fellowship by the Australia Council in 1995. He was the recipient of the Lawrence O'Shaughnessy Award 2000, the first poet in Irish to achieve that distinction. A bilingual collection *Ag Greadadh bas sa Reilig/Clapping in the Cemetery* was published by Cló Iar-Chonnachta in 2005, and reprinted in 2006. His latest collection is *Cúpla Siamach an Ama* (*The Siamese Twins of Time*) published by Coiscéim in December 2006. A second bilingual volume *agus rud eile de/and another thing* will be published in 2009.

POETRY COLLECTIONS

Próca solais is luatha. (1988). Baile Átha Cliath, Coiscéim.
30 Dán. (1992). Baile Átha Cliath, Coiscéim.
Aimsir Bhreicneach/Freckled Weather. (1993). Canberra, Leros Press.
Gobán Cré is Cloch/Sentences of Earth and Stone. (1996). Melbourne, Black Pepper Press.
Seo. Siúd. Agus Uile. (1997). Baile Átha Cliath, Coiscéim.
Corcach agus Dánta Eile. (1999). Baile Átha Cliath, Coiscéim.
Cork and Other Poems. (1999). Melbourne, Black Pepper Press.
agus rud eile de. (2002). Baile Átha Cliath, Coiscéim.
Ag Greadadh Bas sa Reilig/Clapping in the Cemetery. (2005). Conamara, Cló Iar-Chonnachta.
Cúpla Siamach an Ama. (2006). Baile Átha Cliath, Coiscéim.

Sméara Dubha

Priocann sí braonta fola den sceach,
súile daite chomh glé
leis an am le teacht
nár dhoirchigh a hóige go fóill.

Más buan mo chuimhne, adeir sí,
bliain tar éis filleadh ón iasacht,
níl na sméara chomh blasta in aon chor
le sneachta na bliana seo caite.

Tá gile na taoide
chomh hard leis an ngrian
a líonann gach cuas dá cuisle,
is dealg sa chaint i ngan fhios di
a réabann craiceann mo mhéar.

Ba mhaith léi go mblaisfinn
den mhilseacht dhubh
atá chomh searbh
leis an bhfírinne ghlan
ar bharr mo theanga.

Ó thabharfainn an lá seo
is na laethanta gearra go léir
a tháinig roimhe dem shaol
ach greim scrogaill
a bhreith ar an uain,

go mblaisfeadh sí arís is arís eile
de sholas an lae seo ag dul as
chomh ciúin le sneachta na bliana seo caite
nár bhuail (is nach mbuailfidh)
urlár an tsaoil seo go deo.

Blackberries

She pricks blood-drops from a bush,
eyes lit bright
as time to come
that hasn't yet darkened her days.

If I remember rightly, she says,
a year after coming back,
the blackberries aren't nearly as sweet
as last year's snow.

The white of the tide
is bright as the sun
that fills every cave in her heart,
and a thorn in her talk, unknown to her,
skins the tips of my fingers.

She wants me to taste
the black sweetness,
that is bitter as truth
on the tip of my tongue.

If I could take this day
and all the little days
of my life, now gone,
I would, take time by the throat,
and choke it until it stopped

so she could taste time and again
the leaving light of this day
silent as last year's snow
that never fell (nor will fall)
upon this earth.

Cranndacht

Chuir sí crann caorthainn
sa ghairdín inniu

chuimil a préamhacha
sular neadaigh i bpoll

méara chomh slim
le duilliúr an chrainn

a roghnaigh sí
dem bhuíochas.

    Fiúise, ar ndóigh,
    a bhí uaimse,
    cloigíní fola,
    deora Dé.

Is fada léi, a deir sí,
go bhfásfaidh an crann
go dtí an fhuinneog i mbarr an tí
mar a gcodlaíonn sí,

smearadh cré
ar a lámha leonta cailín
is iníon rí Gréige ag siúl
na hallaí bána laistiar dá súil.

    Tá rian fola
    ar stoc an chrainn
    ina diaidh
    nach féidir
    le máthair na báistí
    a ghlanadh ná a leigheas.

Nuair a éiríonn an fhuil
i ngéaga an chaorthainn
dem bhuíochas, braithim
an chré ag análú go trom
sa seomra codlata in aice liom.

Go domhain san oíche
ionam féin, goileann Dia
racht fiúisí os íseal;
ní féidir a thocht a mhaolú.

Trees

She planted mountain
ash in the garden today

teasing the roots
before easing them
into the earth

fingers as slender
as the leaves of the tree

she chose herself
in spite of me.

> I wanted fuchsia,
> of course,
> bloodbells,
> Godtears.

She can't wait, she says,
for the tree to grow high
as the topmost window
where she sleeps,

earthstains on her torn fingers
and a Greek king's daughter
walking the white halls
behind her eyes.

> She's left a bloodstain
> on the bole of the tree
> that the rain's mother
> can't clean or heal.

When the blood rises
in the arms of the mountain ash
in spite of me, I feel
the earth breathing heavily
in the bedroom next to mine.

In the dead of night
in me, God cries
buckets of fuchsia
so quiet that no one
hears his grief without end.

Comhcheilg na Súl

Tá a pictiúr sa pháipéar ar maidin,
an cailín
atá ar iarraidh le seachtain.

Féachann sí orm
mar a d'fhéach, ní foláir,
ar an té a ghlac an grianghraf,

cara dil
nó leannán fir, adéarfainn,
ó loinnir na comhcheilge
ina súil,

féachann sí orm
le hiontaoibh shoineanta iomlán.

Braithim, ina dhiaidh sin,
míshocracht éigin os cionn a gáire,
imní ag bordáil le cúinne a béil
mar a bheadh leide faighte aici roimhré,
roimh chomhcheilg na súl
as a dtarla sí féin,
gur ghearr a ré.

Níl aon dealramh aici,
dubh, bán ná riabhach,
le héinne dem chlannsa iníon.

Ach tá Dia ar iarraidh
le seachtain
is ní féidir liom
féachaint go cruinn

ar na hógmhná
codlatacha im thimpeall
aimsir bhricfeasta
a bhfuil dealramh ina ngné acu
leis an té is ansa liom sa tsaol.

Cuirim páipéar na maidine
idir mé
is an mhuinín
shoineanta iomlán
a chím ag stánadh orm
as a súile dorcha gan scáth.

Conspiracy of Eyes

Her picture is in the morning paper,
the girl
who's been missing for a week.

She looks at me
like she must've looked
at the one who took the photograph,

a close friend,
or boyfriend, I'd say,
from the hint
of mischief in her eyes.

She looks at me
with complete misplaced confidence.

And still I feel a jitter
hanging over her smile,
worrying the corners of her mouth
as if she'd got some inkling,
before the conspiring of eyes
from which she was born,
she wasn't long
for this world.

She looks nothing at all
like any of my daughters.

But God
has gone missing
for the past week
and I can't look too closely

at the drowsy young ones
at their breakfast beside me
with a likeness in their looks
to the one I love the most.

I put the morning paper
between me
and the complete
misplaced confidence
that stares me out
from their dark eyes unafraid.

Translations by the author with Mary O'Donoghue
and Kevin Anderson.

'The brindled cat is chewing the nightingale's tongue'

For R.S. Thomas, reading a poem in translation was 'like kissing through a handkerchief', a promise of intimacy simultaneously offered and withheld, a pleasure partially consummated, endlessly deferred, deflected, postponed.

Gerry Murphy's poem on 'Translation and its discontents' from which the title of this essay is taken is a reminder of the more destructive aspects of translation. In this case, the translator appropriates material from another language to sustain the appetite of his own, devouring the original in the process.

Most commentators agree that translation is as impossible as it is necessary. The original remains obstinately, shyly, out of reach, and yet the impression it leaves on the linguistic veil that both conceals and reveals confirms the marvellous diversity of languages other than our own.

The danger of suffocation by translation has led to some unease among Irish language poets. Biddy Jenkinson's wish that her poems not be translated into English in Ireland is a 'small rude gesture' on behalf of linguistic diversity, the need to ensure that Irish survives on its own terms.

For myself, I prefer not to publish my work bilingually in Ireland until the poems have reached their first audience among Irish speakers. The creative act of a poem requires that readers alert to the possibilities contained in the original complete the circuit of potential meaning which is opened by the words on the page. The real or imagined reader is a sounding board that enables the poem to resonate within the acoustic of the language in which it is written.

This is not to say that the poem does not contain exotic notes imported from elsewhere but that the echo chamber of the language in which it was written provides readers and writers of that language with a shared acoustic within which the poem can achieve its particular resonance. To introduce an alternative set of possibilities by making a translation available simultaneously with the original is to short circuit that process of signification. The more Irish language readers read in Irish without the artificial life support of English, the more they are attuned to the possibilities of the language, the more amplified the resonance of which poetry in Irish becomes capable.

The decision to defer translation then is a tactical one rather a matter of principle, one that allows breathing space for the original poem to speak and become itself to the full extent of which it is capable before allowing others to speak on its behalf.

Over the past five years, I have worked closely with Kevin Anderson, Biddy Jenkinson, and Mary O'Donoghue on English translations of my work. I had previously published three bilingual collections in Australia, but felt that these were inadequate due to a lack of dexterity on my part in the manipulation of English as a medium for poetry. If my poems were to be rehoused in English, I wanted them to speak as clearly as possible in their second language, to exploit the full range of possibilities available while remaining true to themselves.

It was important that the translators should be able to grapple directly with the original poems rather than relying on me for 'cribs' to work from. The 'crib' is the poor relation, the drudge, in the project of translation, an allegedly 'literal' rendering of one language to another before the real 'creative' work begins. As a recovering cribber my own sense is that the first move is the critical one, the first impression the original language makes on the target language, which provides the template for all subsequent versions.

I am cautious of any translation where the person credited with the work has not engaged directly with the original because she/he lacks the linguistic skills to do so. Two things result from this: the semantic range of the original remains inaudible to the 'translator', while the resources of the target language can not be fully explored by the cribber.

I am fortunate that Kevin, Biddy, and Mary are capable of full engagement with the original poems in Irish, a precondition for successful translation according to Breandán Ó Doibhlinn: 'I can only say that for me, translating a poem means first of all living it to the fullest degree possible in its original language and then reliving it in its new linguistic garb'. In fact, the translators have read the originals sufficiently well to rebuke me for having taken unacceptable liberties with my own work in my earlier English translations!

The litmus test for our translations is that a reader should be able to check the translation against the original and not feel that she/he had been cheated by the transaction. If so inclined, readers should be able to use the translation as a temporary construction that would allow them to make the journey across the page from English into Irish.

The second requirement is that I should be able to read the English versions as if they were my own, rather than a script prepared by others which I stumble over because its accent and style are unsuited to my voice. This requires a considerable degree of self-restraint on the part of translators who are capable of hitting notes in English that are beyond my range. It is a tribute to their discretion that I can hardly tell which of us/them is responsible for individual lines in the English versions of the poems, that I sometimes imagine them to be all my own work.

How long this will last is a moot point. I overhear emailed intimations of mutiny as they wonder aloud to each other whether it would not be unreasonable for readers to accept that my English has improved over time and that I am now capable of striking notes that were previously beyond me, that I am, in fact, a credit to the voice coaches who have trained me. It's time, I think, we discussed again the art and etiquette of hankies, handkerchiefs, if you will.

Anne Fitzgerald
(1965-)

Born in Dublin and grew up in Sandycove, Co. Dublin. She read Law at Trinity College, Dublin and received an M.A. in Creative Writing from Queen's University, Belfast. She has edited, produced and designed four anthologies of young adults' poetry *The Colour of the World*, *The Compass* (Dublin, MET Press, 2003, 2004), *Uncharted Voyage* and *Deep Canyons* (Dublin, Loreto Abbey Dalkey Press, 2004, 2005). She founded MET Press and Loreto Abbey Dalkey Press. She is a recipient of the Ireland Fund of Monaco Writer-in-Residence bursary at The Princess Grace Irish Library in Monaco.

POETRY COLLECTIONS

Swimming Lessons. (2001). Wales, Stonebridge Press.
The Map of Everything. (2006). Dublin, Forty Foot Press.

Tattoos

A scent of bean sprouts interned in our hot
press meets me like a wall of foreign heat,

between cheesecloth underwear and linen
pressed by our very own Swastika Laundry. *

From the warmth of darkness eyes peek
out. Shy pupils huddle moisture, scrum-like,

caught in the large curve of a glass thick
jamjar. Strain water through muslin daily,

leave no excess, enough to breathe, so says
instructions got from the Dandelion Market,

top of Stephen's Green where U2 gigged free,
amongst belts, buckles and bows going for

a song, a fraction of Grafton Street's, ran circles
round punters squaring the Green as if thrown duck

crusts, foreshadowed by Newman's cardinal eye,
and distant music echoes Harcourt St. train tracks.

In the absence of light, pulses beat behind timber
doors. Oświęcim language draughts grow silently.

---

* In Dublin, Ireland, a laundry company know as the Swastika Laundry
existed for many years in Dartry and Ballsbridge (both on the River
Dodder on the south side of the city). It was founded in 1912 and
remained in business until the late 1960s.

Ditched

You are beside yourself, as he gives you bullet and elbow
in one breath, without bye or leave, leaves you to your own
devices as a loose explosive wire waiting for reconnection.

Signalling through Space without Wires [*]

I happened upon you in Lowestoft, no
less, of all places one might run into

an old flame, who'd managed to turn
me down-side-up, and outside-in.

Took me a good month of Sundays
it did to get over you. It's often not

great to dwell on such matters
that turn into worry beads, leads

it does to all kinds of stuff. Rough
class of dreams can deconstruct day

out of night and night out of day,
in pursuit of black holes and water

on Mars, never mind that broken
engagement you'd thought eternity-

proof. In the pudding is where proof
hid, as you turn out hundreds a-pastry

lids together with young Sid Lipton,
for cottage and shepherd's pie crusts.

Lust they say drove you. Finds it hard
to imagine, even though the charge-

sheet said, *cottaging in public lavatory*,
with a flock of George Michael lookalikes.

Fights broke out in the patisserie the likes
of which I'd not seen since Powell's Rivers

of Blood, back in sixty-eight. And Joan Rivers
providing alternative comedy down Broadway,

away from it all. Calls became far, far fewer
as if watching Marconi's dots and dashes cross

the ocean, then fade into rain. All that electricity
oscillating thoughts as radio waves lost at sea.

* *Signalling through Space without Wires* is the title of a paper by William
Henry Preece (the Chief Electrical Engineer of the British Post
Office) introducing Marconi's work to the general public at the Royal
Institute on June 4th, 1897.

Shoulder to no literary wheel

The year is 1896. Wednesday, January 1st, begins this leap year. Tipperary defeats Dublin in the tenth All-Ireland Senior Hurling Championship. James Connolly establishes the Socialist Republican Party. Harriet Beecher Stowe, Dodie Smith, William Morris and Alfred Nobel pass away. Wilheim Röntgen discovers X-rays, the first edition of the Dow Jones Industrial Average is published and gold is discovered in the Klondike. Oscar Wilde's play *Salomé* premieres in Paris, the Pontifical University of Maynooth is established by Pontifical Charter and Greece hosts the first Olympic Games in the modern era. John Mary Pius Boland, an Irish Nationalist and MP, is the first Irish tennis Olympian medallist. Mark Twain publishes *Tom Sawyer* and *Detective*, Theodore Roosevelt's final volume of *The Winning of the West* is released and William Morris's *The Well at the World's End* finds its readers. In Dublin, Dan Lowery's Music Hall screens its first cinema shows. Also these twelve months mark the births of the Irish stage and screen actor, Arthur Sheils, the poet and theatre director, F. R. Higgins, author Liam O'Flaherty and the poet William Monk Gibbon, who was largely overshadowed by his contemporary, Austin Clarke. It is to Monk Gibbon that I wish to turn.

William Monk Gibbon was born in Dublin on 15th December, 1896. His father was a Church of Ireland clergyman and vicar of Taney parish, Dundrum from 1900, where W.B. Yeats's sisters Lily and Lolly were parishioners. Coincidentally, Yeats and Gibbon were related. Monk Gibbon was educated at St. Columba's College, Rathfarnham and Keble College, Oxford. He was a prolific poet, novelist, biographer and critic. From 1914-1918 he served in World War I until he was invalided out. His autobiography *Inglorious Soldier* (1968) recounts his war experiences. He taught in various schools in Wales, Switzerland and Dublin until well into his seventies. Accounts of which he drew upon for two of his five autobiographical novels *Mount Ida* (1948) and *The Pupil* (1981); discussing love affairs of school-teaching days and platonic love for a schoolgirl respectively. Gibbon was regarded as an AE (George Russell) scholar. He was also a member of the Irish Academy of Letters and a Fellow of the Royal Society of Literature. In 1928 Gibbon married Winifred Dingwall and they had six children.

Gibbon is possibly best remembered for his critical biography of Yeats *The Masterpiece and the Man: Yeats as I knew Him* (1959) and *Yeats's Earlier Poems* and *On Re-reading Yeats*. These critical accounts of Yeats seem strange, considering he had previously written to Gibbon telling him that he had found his voice. Gibbon published six poetry collections *The Tremulous String* (1926), *The Branch of Hawthorn Tree* (1927), *For Daws To Peck At* (1929), *Seventeen Sonnets* (1932), *This Insubstantial Pageant* (1951) and *The Velvet Bow and Other Poems* (1972). In 1928 he was awarded The Tailteann Silver Medal for *The Branch of Hawthorn Tree* (1927). Appearance-wise the Picart Le Doux illustrated edition of this collection visually gives the poems a more weighted rendering towards Victorian nursery rhyme books. His *Seventeen Sonnets* reflects upon his admiration for English Georgian verse.

Gibbon was a lyric poet with a keen eye for traditional

form. His poems are not rooted in place like those of his contemporaries. His preoccupations are usually of an uncomplicated nature with a reflective nod towards classical erudition. Thematically his poems are often charged with a metaphysical religiosity, discussing Truth, Beauty and Destiny. His language possesses an archaic nineteenth-century loftiness in such poems as *The Charge*. On other occasions his language is simple and straightforward, leaving readers searching for irony or metaphor, not obfuscated by existence. Nonetheless, there is a fluent flamboyance to his poetry that is designed perhaps for a more acoustic appreciation than that of an interpretative one at times. Gibbon writes candidly, if scathingly about poets and what their job is. In *Of Other Poets, Dispossessed Poets, and Poets* he says 'more and more, poets grow/ less and less like their task'. [*] By his own admission Gibbon stated that he had never put his shoulder to any literary wheel.

In 1987 U2 released *The Joshua Tree*, unprecedented queues lengthened outside the American Embassy in Dublin and the Northern Ireland Troubles were at their height. William Monk Gibbon died on October 29th. He belonged to that refreshing age of poetry where great anticipation preceded publications of long-awaited slim volumes, and, when attending infrequent poetry readings were occasions to be savoured long after the events – and the commercial endeavour of facilitating creative writing classes the length and breadth of the country had not yet become an epidemic.

[*] *The Velvet Bow and Other Poems* (London, Hutchinson, 1972),
   Poets. p. 86.

Leontia Flynn
(1974-)

Born and grew up in Co. Down, Northern Ireland. She was awarded an M.A. from the University of Edinburgh and a B.A. and Ph.D. (thesis on the poetry of Medbh McGuckian) from Queen's University, Belfast. She won a Gregory Award for her poetry in 2000 and The Forward Prize for Best First Collection in 2004. In 2008 she won both the Rooney Prize for Irish Literature and a Major Individual Artist Award from the Northern Ireland Arts Council. She now lives in Belfast and is a Research Fellow at the Seamus Heaney Centre for Poetry at Queen's University, Belfast.

POETRY COLLECTIONS

These Days. (2004). London, Jonathan Cape.
Drives. (2008). London, Jonathan Cape.

Art and Wine

In our half-baked Belfast demimonde,
another evening drank itself down neat.
Through the greasy streaks and smears
of a westward third-floor window
I watched as the leaves blew in circles on College Court.

How long, I wondered, would my years blow in circles?
How long could I keep
the dreamed black wave from breaking on the shore?
And would you, I mused, perhaps understand me more,
if I could, for a single second, shut the fuck up?

The Girl Upstairs

The girl upstairs has begun once more to cry.
Her tears won't have the wild momentum of a child's.
They're regular, rhythmic; actually it's kind of soothing
to hear her sob. Outside the rising wind
rumbles the bins and makes the drinkers shout.

I know her cries will ease at one or two.
I know her movements, I know when she comes and goes
twitching the blinds or scrabbling for mail in the hall.
I know her room is haunted by the moon
of a paper lampshade. *I am the girl upstairs.*

The Vibrator

When you had packed up all your books and clothes
and taken the last crap poster down, and walked
like a mournful ghost through the blank, familiar rooms
a thought struck – clang! – loud as a two pence piece
in a metal bucket: where was the vibrator?

Oh cruel Gods! Oh vulgar implement
that was stowed discreetly on some shelf or cupboard
but has almost certainly not been boxed away ....
Oh dirty gift of doubtful provenance
Oh gift – surprise! – for the next week's settling tenants.

Oh nice surprise for next week's settling tenants,
four Polish men paid peanuts by the hour
– for in Belfast too world history holds its sway –
to find alone in some nook or niche-hole the vibrator
still beats, in the dark, its battery-powered heart.

Poetry and Work

I am a research fellow at the Seamus Heaney Centre for Poetry at Queen's University, Belfast. The Heaney Centre is part of the English department which teaches not reading or criticism but writing – there are M.A. courses in Creative Writing focusing on both prose and poetry – and we also invite prominent authors to the centre to read from their work. My position there, however, straddles the academic/creative divide. Five years ago I completed a Ph.D. thesis on poetry and in the same year I published my first collection of poems *These Days*.

When I left school fifteen years ago (which sounds longer than it feels), I didn't want to do anything other than write. At the time, though, unlike seeking to become an accountant or a lawyer, there didn't seem to be any formal training available for this – just trial and error and extensive reading. Since publishing a book, I know some people writing poetry who eke out a living on grants, awards and (mainly) teaching, and in a way poetry has become increasingly professionalized and university based. However, my initial sense that poetry wasn't exactly a career didn't arise from the insubstantiality of the salary so much as from the essentially precarious and mysterious nature of how poems get written. In my case this is rarely and unpredictably. To say that it is one's job to write poems, therefore feels to me like saying it is one's job to have mood swings.

Subsequently, it has always seemed important to me to do something else as well — and my something else was to remain at university or return there after a series of terrible part-time jobs. The academic work I try to do is something from which I'm relatively detached, which does not feel intimately connected to me. In fact, unless I am actually writing something, I can be ambivalent about it. Poetry however, despite not being a 'job', is more or less always on my mind. Even when I'm not doing it, it is, overwhelmingly, the thing I am not doing. I seem to need an enormous amount of free time in order to write, which usually means neglecting something else. I wrote a lot of the poems in *These Days* during a Master's degree which I found so baffling that, effectively, I gave it up. Despite a popular myth about women, it looks like I am not able to multi-task.

If it were true, as John Keats said, that poetry should come 'as naturally as leaves to tree' or not come at all, I would have stopped trying ages ago. When poetry does not come easily, I wheedle with it in the way people do with children: I make bargains, offer bribes, I threaten to quit. Several prominent poets have normalised writing poetry as just another kind of trade, but although a lot of it can be learned I think, frankly, that you have to be a bit strange to want to do it. I often feel as though I have a kind of inconvenient, slightly embarrassing compulsion which I almost never discuss socially.

Publishing confronts you with the fact that your ideal reader does not exist. You probably need to be thick-skinned to publish and yet I suspect, temperamentally, people who write poetry are not thick-skinned. Criticism can be awful, and even praise can be strangely upsetting when it seems misdirected or patronising. Complete strangers will contact you to say they have nominated you for an award, then contact you again to tell you they have decided not to give it to you. It feels like walking into a room, having done your best to look presentable, and finding yourself being given a detailed breakdown of the various good and bad features of your appearance. Yet all of this is more than rewarded by the moments when something goes right, and a poem unfolds itself. Quite simply, this gives me more pleasure than anything I know.

Margaret Galvin
(1959-)

Born and grew up in Cahir, Co. Tipperary. She was educated locally and at University College, Cork and has lived in Wexford since 1979. She worked for a number of years with the library service before moving to *People Newspapers* where she was appointed editor of the weekly magazine *Ireland's Own*. She resigned in 2000 to concentrate on writing, storytelling and bringing up her son, Ibar Quirke. Her poetry has been published in *Poetry Ireland Review*, *The SHOp*, *Southword*, *Iota*, *The Bath Studies Review*, *The Red Wheelbarrow*, *Brand* and *Poetry Cornwall*. In 2003 she was awarded The Brendan Kennelly and Smurfit Samhain prizes. She was also a prize-winner in the Padraic Fallon Memorial Competition in 2008. Her poetry has been described by Anne Le Marquand Hartigan as 'sharp, clear and unflinching'. Fred Johnston has said 'Galvin collides head-on with experience as sieved through story-telling and narrative'.

POETRY COLLECTIONS

Miresuck And Slaver. (1989). Gloucester, Tuba Press.
Habitual Keeper. (1993). Gloucester, Tuba Press.
The Waiting Room. (2005). Kerry, Doghouse Books.
The Wishbone. (2007). Wexford County Council Public Library Service.

Service

The sacristan in Saint Paul's
baroque church works all day
in the hush of this dark interior.
Quiet amongst the icons and treasures
he buffs the candlesticks to glossy lustre,
burnishes the silver with his breath,
checks his reflection in the gleam.

In his soft shoes he glides
through the nave and aisles,
genuflects before the venerated
remains in the glittering reliquary.
Over him the ceiling frescoes
are florid, the dome rococo.

On feast days he simmers
lemon rind and cinnamon sticks
until the heady musk wafts
through the gilded plaster and marble,
pervades the internal architecture.

His home is cool and plain and spare,
the surfaces ceramic. His wife is careful
with the light cottons he favours
in this Mediterranean heat,
mindful of his preference
for lamb stew, the sweet tooth
she satisfies with honey cake.

The Legacy

Lady Florence Dixon addresses me by e-mail as dear.
I warm to her old-world courtesy,
the calmness with which she introduces herself
as a dying woman, drawing down
her last will and testaments in cyberspace,
directed by God Himself, to favour me
as sole beneficiary of her fortune:
three million, five hundred thousand euro.
And while I'm free to do with it what I choose,
she urges me, in reserved and cultured tones,
to consider the motherless and less fortunate.

And for a moment I'm tempted to contact
Pedro Antonio Abagado, the lawyer appointed
to transfer these unexpected gains.
An impeccable advocate, she assures me,
who will observe confidentiality
until this delicate and unusual transaction is complete.
A Latin gentleman, solemn as an oath, who specialises
in wills, bequests and all manner of inheritance.
A professional to his manicured fingertips
who will lodge the legacy in full
on receipt of the relevant banking details.

Beauty Kit

When Tom Corbett, the roadman,
set his cap at Aunty Kit, she became
a sort of kitchen table beautician.
She'd prop a shard of mirror glass
against a milkbottle, inspect herself
in the mottle and mist, isolate the grey
strands at her temples.
A jug of tea cooled at her elbow
to coat the wiry whiskers
of middle-age with tannin.
The poker reddened in the fire
to corkscrew her hair with kiss curls,
the crimps and spirals stiffened
with a paste of sugar and water.

The grit and crystals of soot and wood ash
from the grate whitened her teeth.

Her cheeks and lips were rouged
with aniseed balls:
she'd suck the shiny, red-brown gobstoppers,
rub the spit into the sag and wrinkle
of crows' feet and worry lines.
Hope that Tom Corbett, the roadman,
would relish the sweet
and aromatic liquorice of her face.

Poetry as personal reclamation

According to the American poet Jane Kenyon, 'one of the functions of poetry is to keep the memory of people, places, things and happenings alive'. This is very much what I set out to do in much of my writing, to evoke an era, resurrect and preserve memories of individuals, locations, occurrences and objects.

I was especially fortunate, through the sponsorship of Wexford County Council Library Service, to be able to devote a whole collection *The Wishbone* (2007) to lyrical narratives, poems that essentially told stories. Conscious of John Steinbeck's view that as human beings we are lonesome creatures, we try to be less lonesome by tapping into one of the ancient panaceas for loneliness, storytelling. For me, poetry and storytelling are inextricably linked. I always work from the starting point of the story, what happened, to whom and to what end. Much of this investigation through story visits the past in the spirit of L. P. Hartley's celebrated remark: 'The past is a foreign country. They do things differently there'. It redraws that rich and varied cast of characters and happenings to full emotional height and weight. Poetry enables me to decipher my personal stories and subject them to closer emotional scrutiny, thereby validating the various identities assumed through the agencies of childhood, death, family life, love, separation – the full multiplicity of experiences and influences that mould us. Childhood is, of course, a particularly rich seam to mine for incidents seminal to poetry. I echo Flannery O'Connor's view that by the time we have reached eight years of age enough has happened to us to write about for a lifetime!

The story is the raw material. The translation of the tale into the pithy, compressed wisdom of poetry is the artist's task. Amongst the many features that render the poem unique and compelling, I emphasise the role of detail. To quote the American laureate Ted Kooser, writing in *The Poetry Home Repair Manual*, 'Memory and imagination are excellent tools when it comes to creating a setting, for example, but it's observed detail that really makes a poem vivid.' It is the specific experience that vivifies the poem with authenticity and authority and enables the reader to intuit the bigger picture and deeper truth that lies behind the work. The value of the specific, concrete observation cannot be over-emphasised. Paying attention to all that surrounds us always pays dividends as larger subjects emerge from sensitively observed particulars. The devil is in the detail as we set about describing and exploring the business of being human through poetry. The more concrete the detail, the more compelling, revealing and resonant the narrative. Nothing convinces like the unpredictable detail lively with its lived ring of authenticity. Nothing persuades like the particular and specific as it renders the poem/story luminous and memorable, evoking in the reader that sense of shared understanding.

Coleridge's view that 'poetry is the best words in the best order' holds as true for contemporary writing as it did when uttered in the Romantic era. Since the poem has to do all its own explaining it is crucial that the engaging anecdote is told through specific word and tone choice. Carefully chosen words enliven and animate as they make for strong and memorable poetry. The advice to energise verbs and nouns is well given but adjectives, used sparingly and with precision, can serve to modify the noun and point the reader in the poem's intended direction. According to the Serbian proverb, *Time and patience turn the mulberry leaf to silk.* As poems are revised and redrafted towards clarity and freshness, the ordinary world contained therein is rendered heightened and compelling, as language is fully harnessed in the service of communication.

Ultimately, for me, poetry is about giving shape to experience and emotion and the communication of this through careful artistry. To paraphrase Seamus Heaney the aim of the poet and poetry is to be of service, to ply the effort of an individual's work into the larger work of the community as a whole. The poet is therefore no fey resident of an ivory tower but a robust work-a-day type you'd rub shoulders with on the bus. His/her work is not some remote and lofty activity but a gritty business akin to the work of any smith.

Alan Gillis

(1973-)

Born and grew up near Belfast. He currently lives in Scotland, where he is a lecturer in English at the University of Edinburgh. His first book of poetry *Somebody, Somewhere* was shortlisted for *The Irish Times* Award and won The Rupert and Eithne Strong Award for Best First Collection in 2005. His second book *Hawks and Doves* was a Poetry Book Society Recommendation and was shortlisted for the T. S. Eliot Prize. As a critic, he is author of *Irish Poetry of the 1930s* (Oxford University Press, 2005) and is currently co-editing *The Oxford Handbook of Modern Irish Poetry*.

POETRY COLLECTIONS

Somebody, Somewhere. (2004). Co. Meath, The Gallery Press.
Hawks and Doves. (2007). Co. Meath, The Gallery Press.

Clouds

Bright light sprawling white cotton clouds
look they've never heard of rain:
some see in them faces, memory shapes,
continents, maps of dreams, gondolas
lazing through sunstreams. I mostly see sheep
grazing in a greener-than-green field
bedizzled by buttercups carpeted down
to a fizzing hedge, stone path and two
apple trees standing sentry to a view
of the lough, coastline, chopped open sea,
oblivious to things that might have been
or might be, passing lives, the mist and creep
of stolen thoughts, the dead and unborn
drifting, on their backs, counting sheep.

With or Without You

Oh no, she's listening to Yoko Ono.
We were as well-matched as bread
and milk, as Brian Eno and Bono,
but now I'm hanging to her by a thread,
a terminal patient hooked to a drip.
Now my pet names for her are *shit* and *smack*
and I live for a hit: to lick those lip
glossed lips, be a Moog she might play.
Imagine a millipede on its back,
its thousand legs twitching every which way –
that was my mind when she said her muse was sick
and she was off to discover new music.
Now our love is a derelict studio
where I sit, solo, counting in: *uno, duo* …

The Cloud

On better days he'd fray at the seams,
bits of him floating hither, others thither,
edges wisped and whispered, funnelled and curled,
tentacles feeling for the way the four winds
were blowing. Later he'd turn to hyacinth
or cotton balls doused in China-rose nail
polish on a flasket of lemon and blue.
On his best days a big hole would open
in his chest and a stairway to marvels
would spotlight through. But mostly he'd be
heavy pregnant, gathering his bits together
in a bloated, grimaced and grave-bellied swell
fit to split open a black harvest of grain:
head-hung children who would forbear the rain.

Poetry doesn't exist

Poetry doesn't exist. There's only poems. Very rarely would someone ask what you think about song. They're more likely to ask about a song, or set of songs, or singer. On song, it's hard to get beyond 'yeah, I like it' or 'nah, not for me'. But regarding a song, or set of songs, or singer, you can get straight to business.

Earlier this year I found myself at a primary school near Edinburgh, to judge an annual competition in which ten year olds recited Burns poems they'd learned by rote. I was to note how well they'd memorised the poem, the style of their oratory, and their level of audience awareness. But I was caught on the hop by an unexpected question and answer session. On the dreaded 'now, has anybody got a question for a poet?', I expected fidgety silence, yet was delighted by a forest of raised arms. I felt buoyed by this passion for the poetic. The teacher turned to one boy who seemed particularly keen to ask a question before anyone else (although they all looked about to erupt). 'Well Sam, what have you got to ask the man about writing poems?' The smile on Samuel's face was bright as a banana: 'Mister … would you not rather play football?'

According to W. H. Auden, you're only a poet at the moment you're making a last revision to a new poem. The moment before, you're still only a potential poet. The moment after, you're someone who has ceased to write poetry, perhaps forever. This seems an insightful excuse for most poets' discomfort when talking about poetry-in-general in public (it's so easy to try too hard, and be full of hot wind and affected bluster; or not try hard enough, and be blasé or pig or empty-headed). According to Auden, a so-called poet won't really know what he or she is talking about, because they're not, when speaking of poetry, a poet. And, as we've agreed, there's no such thing as poetry anyway.

As it happens, poetic discourse finds its best room to bloom in the ritualised spaces of the seminar or classroom, as well as in the voluntary corners of private conversation. In one instance, you do a formal job; in the other, you talk freely because you want to. The key to both is that there tends to be focus. But if we were to ban all talk of poetry, and talked about poems or poets instead, this might help disintegrate the generalised sense of preciousness and effete specialisation with which the art is regarded throughout culture at large, so that verse might truly open its doors to the lives of those it is written for (i.e. everybody).

Anyway, I bring this up because I'm starting to think Auden's truism isn't true. Technically, a footballer is only a footballer for the ninety minutes of the game. But a professional will spend all day warming up, warming down, dribbling, being massaged, having jacuzzis, watching games, shooting, running round in circles, standing still for three minutes while being measured by a tailor, signing photographs of himself, and so on. Now, we'd be extremely pedantic if we insisted that while doing these adjunct activities, he was merely a warmer-upper, warmer-downer, dribbler, massagee, jacuzzeur, spectator, shooter, ring-runner, dummy, narcissist and so on. Instead, we recognise a footballer doing footbally things.

By the same rationale, we should acknowledge that to get to the point of being a poet (making a last revision to a new poem), a person must do a lot of other things. First and foremost, he or she must live (I mean in the vastly time-consuming mundane put the bread on the table the same as everybody else sense). After that, he or she must spend as much leftover time as possible reading, remembering things, forgetting them again, making things up, sitting about, walking about, lying about, reading, getting wrecked (optional), listening to music, listening to the wind, eavesdropping, reading, being an all-round right royal pain in the arse (optional), sky-watching, picture-watching, wall-watching, reading, nonsense-jotting, note-scribbling, paper-ripping and reading. And that's before we mention the all-important and constant apprenticeship to words in pattern. So, let's face it, being a poet is a full-time job.

Without a doubt, much of the time I'd rather be playing football. But then again, much of the time I'd rather be winning the lottery or getting intimate with Eva Mendes. However, it's unlikely any of these would match the sensation of finishing a decent poem (I'm only speculating). Certainly, at the primary school near Edinburgh, the kids were great. Words charged with pattern came to life (in a variety of life forms) in the mouth and in the mind. Fun was had. Doors were opened. Goals were scored. It was poetry.

Kevin Higgins
(1967-)

Born in London, he grew up in Galway city where he now lives. With his wife Susan Millar DuMars, he co-organises the Over The Edge literary events in Galway. He also facilitates poetry workshops at Galway Arts Centre, teaches creative writing at Galway Technical Institute and is Writer-in-Residence at Merlin Park Hospital. He is the poetry critic of *The Galway Advertiser* and was a founding co-editor of *The Burning Bush* literary magazine. His collection *The Boy With No Face* was shortlisted for the 2006 Rupert and Eithne Strong Award for Best First Collection by an Irish poet. He won the 2003 Cúirt Festival Poetry Grand Slam and was awarded a literature bursary by the Arts Council in 2005. He has read his work at most of the major literary festivals in Ireland and at a wide variety of venues internationally. Kevin Higgins' work is discussed in poet/critic Justin Quinn's *Cambridge Introduction to Modern Irish Poetry* (Cambridge University Press, 2008). One of the poems from his second collection, *Time Gentlemen, Please*, 'My Militant Tendency', appeared in the *Forward Book of Poetry 2009*. His work will be featured in the forthcoming anthology *Identity Parade – New British and Irish Poets* (Bloodaxe, 2010).

POETRY COLLECTIONS

The Boy With No Face. (2005, reprinted 2007). Co. Clare, Salmon Poetry.
Time Gentlemen, Please. (2008). Co. Clare, Salmon Poetry.

St. Stephen's Day, 1977

for my mother

Yesterday, in my new football boots I moved
like Kevin Keegan through the silver afternoon.
Today, *Mull of Kintyre* is number one
and the film director Howard Hawks is dead.
I take my football boots off,
am myself again.

You're still a skeleton with all day night sweats.
The doctor, who knows the why of everything
but this, has given you back for Christmas.
Most of the turkey goes leathery in the fridge.
Dad puts the telephone down, tells me
to extinguish the TV. The doctor
wants you back three days early.

Our Ford Cortina cradles you
through late afternoon streets,
all those lit windows and wreaths.
But we don't see them. And nothing is said
as we deposit you at Unit Seven,
Merlin Park Hospital. You at the door
giving a small pale wave. In the near distance
the disused boiler's giant chimney stack.
The rain saying terrible things
as we drive off, that Christmas
you didn't die.

Clear Out

Today it all goes to the dumpster,
my old political furniture:

the broken bookcase called
nationalisation of the banks;

the three legged dining chair called
critical support for the P. L.O.,

the fringed, pink lampshade called
theory of the permanent revolution;

the collapsed sofa-bed called
excuses we made for Robert Mugabe;

the retired toilet seat called
the trade union movement.

And the man who spent
twenty five years sitting on it?

At three thirty six pm
in the stripped living room

I forget him. As of now
he never existed.

I'm too busy watching
the delivery man unload

frightening, new furniture
from that van pulled up outside.

Ourselves Again

In the park our ice-lollies
fall victim to the June bank holiday heat,
while in glass rooms numbers moving
through dark computers
declare the future
finished.

Tomorrow, we'll have our double glazing
taken out; the crack put back
in the ceiling and a draught
installed under every door.
I'll attach a For Sale sign
to the seat of my pants.

Gangs of the angry unemployed
will bear down on the G Hotel
chanting "Down with *Daiquiris*
and *Slippery Nipples*! Give us back
our glasses of *Harp*!"

In pubs nationwide, the carpets of yesteryear
will be reinstated, and there'll be meetings
of Sinn Fein The Workers Party
going on permanently upstairs.

On our knees, we'll ask
for the unforgiveness of sins
and life not lasting.
We'll be ourselves again
and then some.

The poetry reading escapes from the Victorian drawing-room

A poetry slam is a competition where poets recite their work, usually for three minutes each, sometimes without the aid of the page. What defines the genre is the foregrounding of performance. At the Cúirt Festival Grand Slam the judges are asked to consider the literary merit of the poem as well as the performance of the poet and the audience reaction. Some have argued that such overt competition is a bad thing. But having your poem (and the way you read it) judged by members of the audience is, surely, just another form of literary criticism. Yes, the wrong poem does sometimes win. However, the poetry reviews which appear in esteemed literary magazines are also on occasion wildly wrong. And as anyone who has navigated its sometimes shark-infested waters will tell you: the Irish poetry scene was already a pretty competitive place, long before the poetry slam set foot here. In her essay *Slams, Open Readings and Dissident Traditions*, Maria Damon argues that in America 'slams have inaugurated some folks into a recent understanding of poetry as a competitive sport (a concept which makes traditionalists uneasy, in spite of the arguably more cutthroat competition for publication opportunities, admission to MFA programmes, and university teaching positions that poison the mainstream 'Creative Writing' community)'.

In Ireland the tradition of poetry, the spoken art, is particularly strong. According to the *Oxford Companion to Irish Literature* "when Lady Gregory and Yeats were gathering folk material in Co. Galway in 1897 and thereafter, they encountered many stories about Antoine Ó Raifteirí (1779-1835) and found that his poems were still sung and recited."

Raifteirí was illiterate and his poems were never written down during his lifetime. As the nineteenth century moved on, Irish poetry found a home in the Victorian drawing room. Raifteirí reciting his verses to peasant ne'er-do-wells gave way to Mr. Yeats reciting his poems to small gatherings of old dears, and not-so-old dears, pausing between stanzas to sip tea from a bone china cup.

The worst contemporary readings, at which the poet reads to five or six people in a hotel with terrible carpet, have their roots in that Victorian drawing room. Although, it has to be said, listening to Yeats's mannered recitation of his great poems in a grand setting was one thing, but sitting there, as A.N. Other mutters or declaims his or her latest to an almost non-existent audience, is a beast of an altogether inferior variety.

For the advocates of this sort of reading, the worst thing in the world would be if people had the temerity to turn up in significant numbers and actually appeared to be enjoying the experience. This would be poetry-become-entertainment and must be stamped out at all costs because, as we learned at school poetry isn't about entertainment, it's about suffering. To them, poetry readings are the literary equivalent of half-eleven Mass on a wet Sunday in Mullingar, without the jokes.

Lately, what Dave Lordan calls 'the live poetry movement' has energised the poetry reading scene by reconnecting Irish poetry with its own oral tradition. At the Over The Edge: Open Readings in Galway City Library there are featured readers with an open mic afterwards. It is not a poetry slam or competition of any type. Many well-known poets have been featured readers: for example Dennis O'Driscoll, Medbh McGuckian and Colette Bryce. But the democratic element which a properly structured open mic introduces has been crucial to the event's success. Several poets who began at the open mic have gone on to be featured readers. A similar openness is also crucial to poetry slams and other new reading series such as Ó Bhéal in Cork and the White House readings in Limerick, both of which encompass an open mic.

A feature of the recent development of the Galway poetry scene has been the central role of workshops. They are not the place to go if you have nothing to declare but your genius. Every word of every poem is open to question. The inclusiveness of the reading scene around Over The Edge and North Beach Poetry Nights is counterbalanced by the seriousness with which these workshops approach the task of helping emerging and beginner poets chisel their poems into the best possible shape. The idea that those who advocate the more populist approach to organising poetry readings believe, as one critic put it, "that all there's to it is to scribble down a mess of 'poetage' on a scrap of paper and yodel it out to an audience, and pretty soon you'll be up there with Paul Durcan and Rita Ann Higgins and Louis De Paor", is a caricature born out of ignorance.

Several poets, with a wide variety of reading and writing styles have begun to emerge from this broad live poetry scene, of which slam is only a part. Poets such as Mary Madec, Neil McCarthy, Celeste Augé, Dave Lordan, Gary King, Elaine Feeney, Ed Boyne, Noel Harrington, Mags Treanor, John Walsh, Miceál Kearney, Billy Ramsell and Lorna Shaughnessy.

The cliché performance poet – the might-have-been

rock-star in the leather-jacket, who instead of availing of the appropriate psychotherapy, leaps around the stage, making what sounds like animal noises – does have some truth in it. I've met him. And I think I've met his brother. But in Ireland, he is not the norm.

Open readings are an import, yes, but so was the sonnet, imported as it was into English from Italy by Thomas Wyatt in the sixteenth century. Poetry is forever hybrid, never pure. The transformed poetry reading scene is helping Irish poetry finally shake off the legacy of that Victorian drawing room. And in the process will perhaps liberate us from what Dave Lordan, the Dublin-based winner of the 2005 Patrick Kavanagh Award and the 2008 Rupert and Eithne Strong Award calls, 'the dictatorship of the one page lyric.' There is a fork in the road. The sign going one way says 'Death in a provincial hotel', the sign going the other, 'New life'.

Gearóid Mac Lochlainn

(1966-)

Born and grew up in Belfast. His poetry has won many awards nationally and internationally and has been translated into several languages. He has been Writer-in-Residence at Queen's University, Belfast and the University of Ulster. He was also the subject of a TG4 documentary Idir Dhá Chomhairle (2007). Gearóid Mac Lochlainn has worked with the British Council and the Arts Council of Northern Ireland. In 2007 he was a Fellow at The William Joiner Centre for the Study of War and Social Consequences at the University of Massachusetts, Boston. He received a Major Arts Council Northern Ireland Award for poetry in 2006.

POETRY COLLECTIONS

Babylon Gaeilgeoir. (1997). Belfast, An Clochán.
Na Scéalaithe. (1999). Co. Galway, Coiscéim.
Sruth Teangacha / Stream Of Tongues. (2002).
Co. Galway, Cló Iar-Chonnachta.
Rakish Paddy Blues. (2004). Belfast, Open House.

Mary

Mary worked in Murphy's bar on the corner of Skillman.
Sometimes she'd talk about home. Sometimes New York.
She was going back. Ten years was enough.
More than enough. No one was coming out anymore.
Not since the feckin patriot act, she said. The party's over.

She was good to go, she said. Back to Wicklow.
What'll I do in feckin Wicklow? I can visit me granny, I suppose.
Maybe I'll try Belfast next time. You just never know what's next.
Here is just work, work and more work. If you can find it.
The invisible war, you know. The feckin towers. All of it.

Last job I done was the worst.
I would wake at dawn, grab a coffee and step into the day
which was still feckin dark. Then the subway on the corner
and I'd ride it all the way into town.
I worked in this restaurant, underground!
Under the feckin ground! Like a mole or badger, or somethin.
Workin under the ground. Always in the dark.
Long hours. Workin tables. All day. Every day.
Dusk till dawn and round again. Day in, day out.

Sometimes I wasn't even sure what feckin season it was.
Except winter. The cold. Big snows, like now.
This one day the train was freezing. Heatin was out.
Me teeth chattered and me knees knocked like maracas.

There was this black guy sat beside me and he was cold too.
I remember we were both shivering. Shaking like. This big
    black guy and me.
He was dressed real neat in a blue city suit and mohair overcoat.
Real smart like. I remember I'd noticed how neat he looked.
Just before I fell asleep. He looked like a feckin actor, ya know.
But the train makes me yawn and I'm over and out

and I'm dozed off beside this big black guy.
And I must have slept real deep cos I wake up at the end of the line
open my eyes all dozy, feelin all warm and cosy,
like I was back in bed, and it's like summer again.
I'm all warm and happy and I open me eyes
and I'm cuddled up against the black guy in the mohair coat,
both of us snoozing and snuggled into each other,
me left arm linked in his, the other wrapped across his waist.
And me feckin head is buried in his chest.
And he's wakin up too and starin at me with his big brown
    sleepy eyes
and my lipsticks all over his collar, and we're just staring at each other
for what seemed like feckin ages. Just staring into each other.
Like crazy people. Like we're feckin in love or something.

Then people started to get on the train
and I stood up and I fixed me skirt and hair
and he fixed his coat and grabbed his case.
And we just got up and walked out of the train,
walked right out of there like nothin had ever happened.
Just walked away. And I never saw him again.
I never saw him again, ever. He just disappeared.

She paused. Her eyes drifting towards the open door.

Can you imagine it, she said, softly now,
Me sleeping with this big black guy on a train,
all curled up together like we're in love or married, or somethin?
Me and this big feckin black guy.

And she giggled and blushed and rolled on her heels
like she was tipsy, clinking against the Bushmills bottles on the shelf.
Then we just stood there, quietly, looking out on Skillman Avenue.
The snow had thawed. The sun was up.
A memory of summer was in the streets.
We were in olde New York.
Waiting for the call.

Aistriúcháin Eile

(athinsint ar an mhiotas)

Bhí fear naofa, rónaofa
amuigh ag siúl ar chraiceann na farraige,
go díreach mar a rinne Íosa féin roimhe
nuair a bhuail sé le Barra
is é ag bádóireacht ina bháidín.

Cad é mar is féidir an rud dodhéanta seo
a dhéanamh? arsa Barra.
Cad é mar is féidir siúl ar bharr uisce?

Ní ar bharr uisce atá mé, arsa an fear naofa,
Ach ar mhachaire, lán bláthanna, féir is fálta.
Nach bhfeiceann tú iad, a chara?

Is sin ráite, líon sé a lámha le deora Dé
is spréigh sé na peitil ar an aer.
Thuirling siad ar an bhád is ar ghruaig Bharra,
iad ina luí os a chomhair, ag lonrú;
corcra is dúdhearg,
mar fhíon na Spáinne,
mar fhuil naofa Íosa.

Anois, arsa an fear naofa, Abair liom…
Cad é mar is féidir leatsa, a Bharra,
bheith ag bádóireacht ar mhachaire?

Is shín Barra amach a lámha láidre,
is síos leo láithreach san fharraige sáite,
gur thóg amach bradán beo beathach,
bradán ársa na beatha.

Translation

A man was walking on the water one day,
Just like Christ had done before,
When he chanced upon Barra
paddling by in his currach.

"Hey," cried Barra, "how can you do what can't be done,
how can you walk on the water?"

"But I'm not walking on water," said the man,
"I'm wandering in a field of flowers. Don't you see them,
    my friend?"

And the man stooped, filled his palms with poppies
and flung the flowers into the air.

The petals fluttered down into the belly of the currach
And alighted in the dark curls and tangles of Barra's hair,
Where they glowed deep and dark as blood.

"Now", said the man, " Tell me Barra –
how are you rowing your boat through a field of flowers?"

Then Barra stooped and thrust his hands into the sea
And pulled out an ancient fish
That kicked and writhed against his grip,
And showered them both
In glitters of water.

Johnny Doran

do Aoibh agus James

Johnny Doran (1907-1950) was a famous musician from the Traveller community. He travelled all over Ireland in a horse-drawn wagon in the 1940s to fairs and all sorts of public gatherings. He made only one recording for the Irish Folklore Commission, but his legacy continues to influence each new generation of musicians. His style was uniquely rapid, flowing and highly improvisational. He is buried in Rathnew cemetery, Co. Wicklow.

> *Sea mhaise, dá mbeadh mileoidean agamsa*
> *Ní bheadh Críost gan cheol anocht*
> – Eoghan Ó Tuairisc *Oíche Nollag*

Is sheinnfinn ceol cuisle duit
Ceolta gaoithe lán calláin duit
Ceol cúlstaighre chiorclaigh duit
Dhéanfainn duit ceol

Is sheinnfinn ceol cistí duit
Ceol duillí darach dorcha duit
Ceol cladaigh ceol ceonna
Dhéanfainn duit ceol

Is murar leor é sin
Bhuel is cuma liomalinn
Ní bheidh deireadh leis an cheol seo go deo

Is sheinnfinn ceolta sí duit
Ceol cuisleannach ciúin duit
Ceol casúir ceol bóthair
Is dhéanfainn duit ceol

Ceol cúlchistine ceolmhaire
Is cairde go leor ann
Iad taobh leis an tine
Ag síorbhualadh ceoil

Is murar leor é sin
Bíodh sé go breá binnilinn
Is iomlán gealaí ag gáirí

Is sheinnfinn ceol meidhreach malartach mealltach
Tintreach is toirneach
Is dhéanfainn duit ceol

Comhshondas comhshondach
Le macallaí sna hallaí
Is líonfainn duit málaí
De cheathanna ceoil

Is murar leor é sin
Sure is cuma liomalinn
Beidh an fíor-rud againn ar ball

Johnny Doran

for the Doran family

Johnny played staccato vibrato legato
Rubato shapes of open streets
An' Rakish Paddy blues

An' Johnny played on the beat off the beat of the beat
Regulator syancopated
Rakish Paddy blues

An' Johnny played waterfalls fox chase music halls
Hurley sticks an' horse fairs
Rakish Paddy blues

An' churring tunes of crescent moons
An' buttercups of horses shoes
An' chimin' bells of bluebell blues
He brings the harvest home

An' Johnny played the fancy trill street corner colour spill
Open tight an' free style
Rakish Paddy blues

An' Johnny played short rolls long rolls double rolls
Tipping on the same note
Rakish Paddy blues

An' Johnny shaped silver keys
On metal rimmed wagon wheels
Hammer tapped the anvil
Rakish Paddy blues

An' delight the night with starbright pipes
An' wheels that roll through wreaths of road
An' chained with daisies to 'is chanter
He brings the harvest home

An' Johnny played North Clare, cattle markets, Eyre Square,
Stomp an' champ of dappled mares
An' Rakish Paddy blues

An' Johnny played open roads minor roads cross roads
Dawn chorus campfires
An' Rakish Paddy blues

An' Johnny sang duende the nuances and nooks
Travelling the inner routes
Of Rakish Paddy blues

An' Coppers an' Brass an' The Fermoy Lassies
The Bunch of Keys an' journeywork
An' churnin' breeze into changeling airs
He brings the harvest home

Brings Plenty

This piece is a take on the old role of Gaelic poets as keepers of
lineage and genealogy and also as messengers – wandering bards
bringing the news/stories from one place to another, making
connections and communicating across cultures. It is also about
the social role of the poet. What do you do with the stories that
are given to you and who do you tell them to, and how?

– Tell James McCormack that Brings Plenty is alive and
well and lives in Rapid City. Tell him Brings Plenty is
alive. *Ata kili lila washte.*

It was a wet drizzled Sunday morning in September, main
street, Rapid City, SD. The whole town was shut down till
after noon and I was stumbling around empty streets
looking for coffee and a smoke.

No coffee. I sat on a bench on the corner of Main Street
and lit up a Camel. Brings Plenty came tearing around
the corner with a swagger and a smile wide as the street.
He stopped to welcome me to town. Brings Plenty liked
strangers. He liked to talk. He had served his time in the
Navy, on the Theodore Roosevelt Aircraft Carrier, Repair
Division, CVN 71 US.

– We went off to fight Gaddafi cos they said he was
goddamned commie, he said. I done my time with an

Irishman like you. His name is James McCormack from Donegal. You know Donegal? You know James McCormack?

– Donegal is big, I said.

Brings Plenty laughed.

– McCormack couldn't even speak American. He was like you. I would tell him, 'McCormack how come you can't speak English right? Me, I'm a Lakota Indian and I can speak American better than you can. You should learn American McCormack'.

He laughed loud bells and the drizzle shivered.

– McCormack never learned American though. That was more than twenty years ago, on the Theodore Roosevelt. Long time ago. Now, I sleep here in Rapid City. It gets real cold here too. But I got this old leather coat. My friend says I look like Indiana Jones in this here coat. My mother used to say I looked like a Mexican cos I got this mustache here. She said my father looked like a Mexican too. Me, I don't like them Mexicans. I call them Mexicans Spaniards. The Crow and the Whites called us Lakota snakes, the Sioux. The Great Sioux Nation.

I lit another Camel and Brings Plenty smoked too.

– Me, I am Lakota, Sioux, from Cheyenne River country, back that way.

He pointed back that way and paused for a bit.

– I grew up there and rode horses all day. Shootin and ridin all day. We had good horses when I was a kid. Plenty of horses. Lakota, he rode the horse and he warred.

That's all we done, warred and warred. We warred with the Crow, and later we warred with the whites. We would fight. The Crow were our enemies. Then the Whites were our enemies. We warred good. That's what we done, you know, we made war.

But that was long ago. My father told me there were thousands of us Sioux. All over these parts. Tens of thousands of Lakota on horses. Think of 10 men, he'd say, then 100 men, then 10 times that by 10 again. There were that many of us back then. And we warred. And the men did their thing. And the women done theirs.

When I was a kid, back that way, on the Cheyenne River, I would shoot at them flyin saucers too. The old man said they hovered over the river to get energy from the water. I shot them flyin saucers and hit them too. I shot them suckers good but the bullets bounced off and up they'd go... without a sound. No engine see, not like a car or a plane. Just swishhh and up they'd go. But I warred with them good. You got them suckers back in Ireland?

— I have a friend who talks about them all the time, I said.

— Flyin saucers. That was then. But now that's all over and I sleep here in that alley over there. It's a nice alley. The kids do paintings with cans. But watch the cops, man. You got to be careful, ya know.

If I had a woman it would all be different.

If I had a woman I would get a house and a car and see my kids again.

If I had a woman I would get a job and stop drinking.

If I had a woman it would be different...

But the last woman I had she got locked up for sixty days and I still don't know why. Maybe she was crazy. I don't need a crazy woman.

So now, I sleep here in Rapid City, and it gets cold. If only I could go back home along the Cheyenne River and ride horses again. But there's nothing there now. They are all dead. No family. All gone. Those flyin saucers are probably still there though. I would like to pop at them suckers again. But I got no rifle. I was good with a rifle. But that's gone too. No vehicle. Nothing.

I'm just here and this town don't even have horses. What sort of place is this? A town with no horses. Oh well, *ata kili lila washte*. Things are really good. Maybe one day I will get a woman. A good woman. Not a crazy woman. I drink too much when I'm alone.

When you go home Irish man, walk into Donegal. And You tell James McCormack. Tell McCormack I send this message. You tell him –

Brings Plenty is alive and well and lives in Rapid City

Ata kili lila washte. Things are good.

Things are really, really good.

When I got back home I thought for a while of driving into Donegal. I hadn't been back that way in years. And I thought I should try to deliver the comm. But somehow it seemed a million miles away. And maybe McCormack had never come home.

John McAuliffe
(1973-)

Born and grew up in Listowel, Co. Kerry. He studied English at N.U.I. Galway. In 2000 he won the RTÉ Poet of the Future Award. His first collection *A Better Life* was shortlisted for the Forward First Collection Award in 2002. He has worked as a teacher and lecturer in Cork and London, writes regularly about contemporary and twentieth-century poetry and directed the Poetry Now Festival in Dún Laoghaire from 2003-2007. He now lives in Manchester where he co-directs the University of Manchester's Centre for New Writing and edits the online journal *The Manchester Review*.

POETRY COLLECTIONS

A Better Life. (2002). Co. Meath, The Gallery Press.
Next Door. (2007). Co. Meath, The Gallery Press.

A Midgie

I pick a midgie out of my red wine.
The garden goes greener in the lilac time.
This will go down on the permanent record.
A night is nothing if not its own reward.
The foxgloves corked with bees.
The snail outlining a life of ease.
The black things wait. Or may never show.
That's innocent. I know, I know.

Badgers

During training, on the Cows Lawn, one of the smokers,
a boy from Ballylongford, coughed up blood, black clots of it.
We stood on the sidelines, clear of the awful mess.
This was the time O'Hare, the Border Fox, was on the loose.
That day, arriving home from school, who didn't promise
he'd never ever take a pull again? Not in the school bog,
or in the back way; not in the fag-breaks at the petrol station.
But another rumour released us. It was the farm and badgers:

brock, feral, slow-clawed terror of the ditch and yard,
wind-pissing shit-spreader, emptier of field and house.
Its fellow travellers, like garrulous crows,
swore the opposite, the blood-dregs nothing
to their stone-silent survivor who was ever in the right,
making us and the herd safer. Or so they said, even if
the epidemiologist, barely visible behind the numbers,
predicts a new reservoir, the level critical.

O'Hare could not be found by the guards: that smokeless week,
I stood in the porch (under a new, secure intercom),
rubbing a leaf between my thumb and index finger,
noticing a little movement in a Volkswagen
parked, like it had been all along, down our road,
as if this were a pitch or a garage forecourt and not
a dead end, a river facing it, its animal sentries
unvisited once as those on many another road.

Return

The towns are not so dark that no one enters;
in nearby docks, the nights
advance on empty lots.
Fanatics gather in community centres.

The dry spell is scanned for signs of rain.
The news will consider
the negligent doctor
or who is immune to a variant strain.

In cooler queues, low-slung jeans
date the waspie;
the bright bars are smokefree
as the ocean's photic zones.

The downturn floats the clearance sale:
staff migrate,
the market
anticipates no return; churches fill.

The igloo melts, the deserts spread:
north and south,
a dolphin's found in every port;
new forms of algae feather the tide.

The boats will travel day and night
and some make land.
For the time being, out of mind
is out of sight:

no walk-outs, no wild shouts
from the dawning dark.
Someone organises scouts,
someone cleans up the park.

Giant Forest

I remember the excitement when reading Irish poetry began to coincide with writing poems. It was like stepping out of a downpour. Except it was a bright, warm day, May 1994. I had bought Derek Mahon's *Selected Poems* and something by WS Merwin. I remember the sunshine because I walked from the docks to the Claddagh in Galway city, to the football pitches and back, past the spot where there is now a plaque to Louis MacNeice. I didn't know then about MacNeice's Galway holiday. I bought an ice-cream and I read the Mahon book on Nimmo's Pier that afternoon. I still think of it in a dazzle of sunlight.

At the university, Mahon was presented as the smartest and most modern of poets, Irish but also a bit Frenchified. Hard work, which I was ready for, feeling 'a hunger to be more serious', a hunger which was gratified by the austere cover quote from the leading Irish Studies academic, Seamus Deane. The cover painting, though, Max Ernst's 'La foresta imbalsamata' told a different story: against a terrifying giant forest, a weirdly childish cut-out bird (a figure Ernst called Loplop) seemed to smile out at the reader.

Few other writers write so lightly as Mahon does about serious things, keeping his balance even as he shifts his reader's attention from JP Donleavy's Dublin ('For the days are long − / from the first milk van / To the last shout in the night, An eternity. But the weeks go by / Like birds;

and the years, the years / Fly past anti–clockwise / Like clock hands in a bar mirror') to 'Penshurst Place' ('the iron hand and the velvet glove – come live with me and be my love') and the 'Lost peoples of Treblinka and Pompeii' in his most famous poem, 'A Disused Shed in Co. Wexford'. The poems present readers with a geography and an orientation to that geography, as well as a totally distinctive music, precise and understanding, ironic and cool but attuned to the elemental and mischievous too: 'First there is darkness, then somehow light / We call this day, and the other night'. It's hard to stop quoting these poems, but one other seems to catch the light which breaks across and out of his poems, like it should break out of any poem:

> The sun rises in spite of everything
> And the far cities are beautiful and bright.
> I lie here in a riot of sunlight
> Watching the day break and the clouds flying.
> Everything is going to be all right.

I came to Mahon through 'Irish Poetry', a course taught using anthology and handouts by a young, temporary lecturer whom I would hear, once, enthusing about a Fugazi gig on the lit and littered footpaths of Salthill. If studying English made me cautious for a while about my judgment of poetry, conversations and arguments about music continued with a fervour that remained enthusiastically evangelical. It was easy to have a position on new wave or alternative rock, to discuss with friends the difference between SLF and The Undertones. Discussions that resembled lecture courses as they laid out their argument like a path through the woods. One friend would make a case for Irish rock music: he knew the difference between Mother Records and a major label, made telling discriminations between The Would-Bes and the Forget-Me-Nots, would relate their sound to a genealogy of recent English bands.

That year those conversations, those kinds of conversation, veered away towards Derek Mahon and Seamus Heaney. In the English Society, a mature student read a poem about different kinds of shoes. He was Student Union President a year later. Someone else read a poem about spaghetti bolognese. For us, anthologies of Irish and American poetry replaced friends' 'various' tapes. I made discovery after discovery, then discoveries within each discovery. But there was no *NME* or *Hot Press* or *Q* with potted histories, single reviews and tour photos. The figure of the poet seemed mysterious and ordinary. It was all so private. Who were these people? Had they really spent decades writing these poems? Did they think it was worth it? One of these poets would tell me later about hearing his poem read by an actor on an arts show, a great, startling melodramatic aria of a poem, and the presenter asking, 'Who wrote this? And where is he?' The poet listened to this, vanishing from sight as the programme moved to its next item, continuing to do what he was doing, ironing his daughter's clothes for school the next day, thinking maybe about where a poem begins and ends.

Mary Montague
(1964-)

Born in Fermanagh and grew up in Ederney, Co. Fermanagh. Studied Genetics and Zoology at Queen's University, Belfast. She worked for many years as a teacher. She has recently returned from Lancaster, England to Co. Derry where she lives in the foothills of the Sperrins. She is a long-standing member of the Errigal Writers Letterkenny, Co. Donegal. She works as a creative writing tutor, an A level Biology examiner and is currently studying for her Master's degree in Animal Behaviour and Welfare at Queen's University Belfast.

POETRY COLLECTIONS

Black Wolf on a White Plain. (2001). Co. Donegal, Summer Palace Press.
Tribe. (2008). Dublin, The Dedalus Press.

The Druid Beech

A dense cohort of spruce encroaches
the ancient giant. His gnarled shoulders,
heavy arms, are cloaked with remnants

to fashion a glade of burnished
radiance: garment for a charmed dance
to the season's tune; loss-fired, fall-bound.

Wild

The woods, meadowed with bluebell;
the air, moist with spring.

You turn off-trail to a nettle-guarded
path beaten by generations; stillness;
incipience of the infant day; birdsong
eddying, dampened in the post-dawn.

The only sound brushing your attention,
a rhythmic *shush shush*
of your jeans chafing wet vegetation.

The path troughs. The woods shade deeper,
glaze intermittently with slants of light.

From behind: a sharp rustle,
thudding rush – you spin – *there!* –
blazing autumn-ripe through vernal
green-purple sward, blind to you,
deaf to their own human-confident noise:
foxes! A pair! – ripping the woods'
meditative veil, lusting spring alight –
Scarlet! Golden! Flame! – tearing
down the slope, barely veering
to avoid you. They frisk to where the path
swoops out of sight but, before they vanish,
the follower (likely the male) leaps
onto a bank; pauses; looks back –
that stare of sanity. Then a whisk
of white-tipped russet

and he's gone –
lured,
guiled,
pheromone-high –

leaving you
gulping rank desire,
dazzled by reckless pleasure, the delights
of the body, one's own, another's,

roused, plenished and
wild, wild, wild.

Festive Flourish

The planet slides its slow curve
past the cusp of solstice,
the long swing out of dark.

The woods are damp with lassitude,
frosted with patience. Glinting
with ice-drops, dusted by hoar,
a braid of hazel and willow frays
against the pearl of winter-low sky.

Branches brighten with trinkets,
baubles; the thin conversation
of morsels of birds. Skeins of finches,
titmice, voices seeping, chinking,
flicker among the twigs. Their
darts, sparkles, candle a sapling
with quickness: a native menorah
shining for the promise of light.

Contemporary Irish Poetry

Contemporary Irish poetry is a broad church built on a rich poetic heritage that is itself vast and imposing. I entered the fold as a poet with a background in science whose work is fuelled by an incorrigible biophilia. My take on the contemporary field is inevitably shaped by this locale, both personal and educational, stretching way beyond the Fermanagh village of my origins which, nonetheless, grounds my earliest poetic experiences.

The first 'poetry' that commanded my attention as a child was not that of nursery rhymes, but the outpourings of old balladeers, rebel songs, sung with intense emotion by my Tipperary mother, stranded, as she felt, in the hostile, alien North whose sympatric culture bore only the faintest resemblance to the rich terrain of the Gael she'd left behind. Of course the strong rhythmic melodies impacted, but what I also absorbed with the political ambitions, the popular allegiances, was a nebulous longing for freedom; the lives of my ancestors funnelled into my mother's voice, as public exhortation for endurance, rebellion, overthrow, mutated to private, personal determination. It seemed that the words of these songs were a safe nest for raw emotion. Language itself was an action of agency; the expression of feeling its deepest reward.

The other form of 'chaunting' that inveigled its way into my psyche, was the Rosary: the hypnotic rhythm, the self-naming as a member of the 'banished children of Eve', coalesced with a similar sense of exile and deprivation to that of the rebel songs. There was always that feeling of a lost Eden, that could somehow be reclaimed with sufficient transforming effort, enough genuine redemptive passion. In the meantime, the cadences of communal prayer, its supplication and grief, gave insight into the shamanic power of ritualised language; the possibility of realisation, to an extent, in the moment of utterance.

As a child, however, the Eden I hankered for was neither religious nor nationalist. I grieved Irish Elk above the Irish patriots; meditated on the Pleistocene rather than Christ's passion; longed for the restoration of the Irish wolf before that of the Irish language. Exile, as I experienced it, was within my own human body. The nearest I could come to transformation was to imagine myself into the body of a horse or a wolf. That act of self-shamanism could hardly be said to have much impact on the world around me.

Despite the richness of Irish poetic culture that could have been made available to me, my British education was fairly limited in this regard. For O level, I studied a variety of poets, mostly English, mostly late nineteenth/ early twentieth century. Many spoke to the raw identification I felt for nature; Hopkins, in particular, took me by the throat, the swoop and swoon of his rapture and despair matching my own. I gleaned enough of his biography to feel its dissonances vis-à-vis the intractable demarcations I was reared with: the English Catholic clergyman convert who remained enduringly loyal to the Crown, despite suffering the privilege of *bás in Éireann*. I was seventeen before I was formally introduced to any contemporary Irish poets. I met no women at all.

I missed them. This was double exile, the curse of the second X-chromosome. To pick up a pen and write myself into, out of a poem, was an act of agency beyond me. To discover, in my twenties, some of the richness of female voices available (if, sometimes, rather difficult to find in those pre-internet days) was both liberating and dispiriting. Where had these women been when I was younger? Why were they not part of the 'canon' when they might have helped me negotiate the difficulties of growing into my female body, helped loosen the strangulation of my own voice?

Such questions have been much considered and discussed over the last number of decades. From Eva Gore-Booth to Eavan Boland, they remain important questions. It is however, doubtless, that to a large extent women have moved from being the object to the authors of poetry, as Boland succinctly put it in her wonderful, dazzling *Object Lessons*. And a young woman in Ireland today will at least find some of those female voices; and perhaps know with a little more certitude than I did, that she can claim her own voice within her own female human body.

What I also find interesting about contemporary Irish poetry, in this context, is the number of poets working outside the academy, sometimes alone, often with the support of local (usually, in the way of these things, female-dominated) writers' groups. Something of the communal basis of Irish culture influences these gatherings: the local, the domestic, is central of the work. They also offer an immediate outlet for the work to be heard, for the poet to gain insight into whether what she's offering has meaning for her alone, or speaks to others. Ireland is also blessed with a number of local poetry presses, such as Donegal's Summer Palace Press, which are invaluable in giving local poets, women in particular, the opportunity to have their work presented to others in that magical artefact, the book as tangible object.

In a world, however, where the global impacts on the minutiae of all of our lives, where I find myself debating when to turn on the central heating, not just out of my need for warmth, or concerns about the cost, but because I'm worried about the impact of the resultant carbon dioxide on the atmosphere, we can no longer, if we ever could, dismember the local from the global. There is an obligation on contemporary Irish poetry to look beyond historic and national borders, address larger questions of destruction and extinction.

Something of this, for me, parallels the gradual claiming by Irish women poets of their own subjecthood; writing about nature is no longer seen as a retreat from more pressing concerns. The natural world, vastly diminished though it may be, is newly written as environmental issues have mutated from the lunatic fringe of my childhood to mainstream and frighteningly relevant. Of course nature does not write herself (note the familiar pronoun); but as part of 'her', we can now bring to our poetry what science has taught us about our own animal bodies; the evolutionary and ecological interconnectedness that ties the fate of our species to that of others, and to the planet as a whole.

Ecopoetics suggests that language is humanity's natural habitat; poetry itself, one particularly rich and vibrant niche. It is our responsibility to incorporate into the august tradition of Irish poetry, the transformative insights that biology, ecology, teaches us. Then, in the same way as the rhythms of the old ballads, communal prayer, ritualised and mediated our historical and spiritual experience, poetry may help us negotiate the complexities, the griefs, of our present and immediate future.

Loss is inevitable; the formalised language of poetry may help us endure it.

Kate Newmann
(1965-)

Born and grew up in Co. Down. Poet and editor, among many publications, she compiled the *Dictionary of Ulster Biography*, which was published by Queen's University, Belfast (1994). She won the Allingham Poetry Prize, the James Prize, the Swansea Roundyhouse Poetry Competition and the Listowel Poetry Prize. In 2006 she launched a CD with poems set to music and accompanied by contemporary Irish composers Deirdre McKay, Elaine Agnew and Bill Campbell. Kate Newmann has held residencies for the Arts Council of Northern Ireland and the Down Lisburn Health Trust, has been the director of the Belmullet Writers' Festival and in 2007 was Writer-in-Residence for the Louis MacNeice Centenary Celebration in Carrickfergus, County Antrim.

POETRY COLLECTIONS

The Blind Woman in the Blue House. (2001). Co. Donegal, Summer Palace Press.
Belongings. (2007). Co. Galway, Arlen House.

Piano Man

In April 2005 a young man was found dripping wet, on a beach in Kent.
He spent four months in a psychiatric hospital without speaking a word.

It's selfish, but we didn't want him
to speak or remember his name,
the stranger found wandering
in the darkroom of the night,
dripping like a half-developed photograph
we could all frame inside our longing.

He came into the unit,
labels cut off his dress suit,
like a found manuscript come to light,
like an anonymous score.

While other patients
coloured Easter bunnies
with thick crayons,
he drew a perfect
grand piano.

He made us all make an exception.
The music room was unlocked
and he'd modulate the antiseptic
with Beethoven, Bach, Handel, Chopin, Liszt.

We were all patients
leaning our torsos close up
to the sealed window to hear,
oblivious of how we looked
from the other side of glass.

Sweat poured down his face,
tunes ran into one another
and sometimes he seemed to
be composing on the spot –
modern, dissonant –
pieces of his own making

then they'd resolve into
Handel's Water Music,
or the Moonlight Sonata,
which he hammered out,
rain falling on ocean.

It was hard to tell
if he understood us
by the scutch and slub
of our words,
or what he knew
in the elusive brown minims of his eyes.

Hundreds of mothers wrote
to claim him as a long-lost child
as though the sea had
birthed him again, adult,
from its crazy amniotic,

washing away the truth
of their worst fear,
as piano man played on,
pressing down the soft pedal
of their sorrow.

He could have been anyone:
a radical Czech rocker,
a French street musician,
a Norwegian sailor,
a Hungarian concert pianist.

I think of him
back on his father's farm in Bavaria,
clinging to the rest
before his destiny resumed
in a minor key,
knowing that to be himself
was to be less loved.

The Wild Cattle of Swona Island, Orkney

They've lived there for years
Since the last inhabitants left them
With the island, casting off
Into the fierce conflicting tides.

Two bulls, four calves and six cows
Roam the boggy fields,
Hoof-prints like runes
Across abandoned acres.

Once a year, a vet makes the journey.
He watches them from a distance,
The way a cow rests the bulk
Of her ribcage on the soggy earth

The way the last boat,
Bleached on the rucked shore
Arcs its empty ballast.
The days fall away like rust flakes

Off the useless gates.
The cattle's breath meets the mizzled air
In currents as unreadable
As the ocean's drowning pull.

Wind rough-tongues their eyes and ears
Like a calf being cleaned.
They are the part of us – warm breathing –
That will always return. That never left.

At the Grave of Edith Piaf

She must have always known
that heavy muffle – black
marble on a crowded family grave.
Her raucousness taken up randomly by rooks.

Abandoned by her mother,
all she had was the memory,
the smell of cold cream.

Growing up in the brothel
where her granny was cook,
she leaned into her as fingers
pared fat off cheap cuts,
salted the pale of flaccid chicken skin,
furniture weary of the fleshy barter,
desolate morning cough
as the door closed behind a last client.

There were no staves to limit the falling scale:
her child dying; so many regrets
collapsing harmonies into a dischord
of pastis, cortisone, morphine, alcohol, heroin;
her voice a strident survivor
fending for itself among the body's sodden needs.

She was seventy before she was fifty,
outliving the obituaries written and ready to roll –
no song after death, no life after song.
On stage she slapped her pianist
in the face for losing her, knowing
he loved her too much to leave her
unaccompanied.

Getting my snake, getting my corset and getting my tongue pierced

I was invited to work in schools on a project funded by the Paul Hamlyn Trust, to generate writing around the emotive issues of drugs, sexually transmitted diseases and suicide. I have always found creative writing to be empowering and healing, and I hoped it would serve in this context.

Before the project began it had to be made absolutely clear to the teacher and the students that the information was *sub rosa*, that it would not carry their names and it would not become a topic of conversation. I was not suggesting that any of them were promiscuous or were taking drugs or were contemplating suicide, but that it was happening to their peer group, that we all needed to be informed so that we could make considered decisions – that if it wasn't relevant to them now, it may be relevant at some point, directly or indirectly.

To begin the process of creative writing, and many of the students had never participated in any writing exercise of this kind, we thought of times when we were happy, and times when we were sad:

High

Getting my snake, and the day I met Luke in Art.
When I got my corset and I got my tongue pierced.

Low

When my brother left the house.
When my dog died – I had her all my life.
When my aunt had a miscarriage I was sad.

I had to declare at this point that I did not take recreational drugs, but that some of my friends did, and it seemed that drugs made for a very heightened happiness and a very black sadness over which you had no control. We talked about marijuana, ecstasy, heroin and cocaine, all the information substantiated by newspaper articles, an excellent Horizon programme on television, and internet research. I did not ask the young people to relate their own experiences, but their writing revealed both how informed and how ignorant the thirteen-to-fifteen-year-old students were.

Before broaching the issue of sexually transmitted diseases, we wrote about unwanted gifts that we had received or given.

Unwanted gifts

I gave my mum towels from a hotel.
I didn't want liquorice at Christmas.
I got woolly hats and scarves and gloves which make me itch.
I gave my sister a Christmas present that was old and mine.
I didn't want a World War II coin from my uncle.
I was given, for my birthday, a banana from my granddad who has Alzheimer's.

We discussed chlamydia, gonorrhoea, genital herpes, syphilis, and, reading from the American poet Mark Doty, H.I.V. and AIDS.

Imagine Aids

It is the positive you would like to negative away.
It is the one test you want to fail.
It is the unseen roller-coaster that you can't get off.
H.I.V. is like something holding you down.
H.I.V. is like being trapped inside a collapsing building.

We wrote about fear, worry, anxiety and sanity.

Worry

Worry makes the music of our breathing lose all rhythm.
It keeps our sleep on the edge of a tall cliff.
Worry turns up the volume and makes us panic.

Fear

When all the lights go out.
Flames in the reflection of a dark eye.
Being locked in; mayhem; night time noises.
There is nothing like the fear when you get your hand
or head stuck in something.
It is like a shoal of fish panicking.

In order to broach suicide we wrote about times when we
had been moved by death.

When I was ten in P6 I was in a car with my friends but
the police were chasing a criminal, I don't know who it was
and we crashed into the car. All my friends died in the
crash. The driver and the passenger beside him were okay.
It was a big car – eight-seater – and five of my friends died
right before my eyes.

Last year, I went to two funerals of friends who have
committed suicide.

We wrote a led piece about suicide (one-line answers to a series of questions), and we all contributed to the piece below:

Suicide: Death by Any Other Name

The music of suicide is drums beating slow like a funeral march.
Violins and cellos are the music of suicide.
Always in a minor key with depressing self-hating lyrics.
The music of suicide takes it too far.
A long shriek like feedback from a cheap amp.

Suicide dances alone, slow with jolting movements.
A long lonely waltz off the edge of yourself.
The dance flows into nothing.
Slow and lonely, the dance of suicide is out of time.

Suicide tastes of rust.
It tastes like gritty water.
A bitter, papery substance, stale and cowardly.
Like your own bad breath when you've been sleeping with your mouth open.
It tastes like chewing on broken glass.

Suicide has a real earthy smell.
It smells like a slaughter house, like sewage or a gas leak.
It smells smotheringly musty.

It forgets about the people left behind.
It forgets about reason, about love.

Suicide creates a language of silence.
An unknown inexplicable language.
Like an animal in pain, the language of scream.
No one knows.
A language too late to be spoken.

It is empty of happy.
Suicide is empty of all colours.
Empty of everything that has happened.

It calls to us with a megaphone.
It calls us with a long piece of rope.
It calls us out with a loud teasing hypnotic voice.
It calls to us in the depth of our problems.
Eerie, God, drowning, slow.
It calls us with a whispering only we can hear.
Suicide calls us – it calls us without remorse.

Usually, while facilitating creative writing, I would encourage free-fall: that we all communicate ourselves and take risks with language. The approach to the writing in this case had to be more cautious. The young people with whom I worked were receptive and honest and appreciative, and I was impressed by their sensibility and bravery. The classes were mixed gender, but this was not problematic as I had thought it might be. I felt that something very unique had taken place and that all young people ought to have access to this means of expressing themselves about taboo subjects.

The project did much to convince me that young people are hungry for information about their own bodies and their own mental health – issues which have to be faced head-on and cannot be fudged – and that the community generated by creativity is the perfect medium.

Nuala Ní Chonchúir

(1970-)

Born and grew up in Palmerstown, Co. Dublin. Poet, fiction writer and editor. Educated at Trinity College, Dublin, Dublin City University and N.U.I. Galway. Her bilingual poetry collection *Tattoo:Tatú* (Arlen House, 2007) was shortlisted for the 2008 Rupert and Eithne Strong Award. Her first full poetry collection *Molly's Daughter* appeared in the ¡DIVAS! Anthology *New Irish Women's Writing* (Arlen House). She edited the second ¡DIVAS! Anthology – *A Sense of Place*. Her two short fiction collections *The Wind Across the Grass* and *To the World of Men, Welcome* were also published by Arlen House. Her third short fiction collection *Nude* will be published by the UK publishers Salt, in September 2009.

Nuala Ní Chonchúir teaches creative writing part-time and has won many literary prizes, including the Cúirt New Writing Prize, RTÉ's Francis MacManus Award, the inaugural Jonathan Swift Award and the Cecil Day Lewis Award.

POETRY COLLECTIONS

Tattoo:Tatú. (2007). Co. Galway, Arlen House
Molly's Daughter. (2003). Co. Galway, Arlen House.

Foetal

we are fastened to our bed
you curl to the curl of me
unshaped to a shape that fits

we sleep, curved into one
and my body begins
the slow, good work

work that weakens me,
balloons me with
both hope and dread

then, after three months,
the heartsick, two-letter slip,
from foetal to fatal

Two Children are Threatened by a Nightingale

after Max Ernst

Max Ernst saw an eye, a nose, a bird's head,
a menacing nightingale and a spinning top
in an innocent knot of wood by his bed.

I see faces in the Rorschach-like pattern
of the curtains, a profile of a man,
snoot-nosed and Victorian, condemning us.

I dream I am in South Africa with a former lover,
we dodge bullets and buy postcards
of old houses, we touch each other's skin.

My son, worried by lightning, pulls out
the plugs all over the house; he stands still
at the window, wondering if airplanes will fall.

And I do not dare to tell him that airplanes do fall,
that people condemn, and that there is menace in more
than paintings of children threatened by a nightingale.

Vanity

Narcissus trumpets his pleasure with himself –
if only to himself – nodding over the lake,
bowing down before his own reflection.

His image is mottled by water-scurf and flies,
like the foxing on an ancient mirror
where mercury and tin have slipped apart.

And soon his yellow freshness will slip too,
leaving a blemished likeness to gaze at, to question.

The Art of the Body:
poem as female self-portrait

For a long time I have wondered about the notion of writers influencing other writers. If I enjoy another poet's work – say Eavan Boland's or Sharon Olds's – does that automatically mean I am influenced by them? I have preferred to think that I engage with and enjoy their work, rather than that I am influenced by it. If influence is really a form of homage or even imitation, is that why I resist the idea of it? I think I have wanted my work to stand on its own and be original without acknowledging the influence of others. Maybe I have been fooling myself.

I distinctly remember the sharp intake of breath when I first read Eavan Boland's orgasm poem, 'Solitary' where no one sees the narrator's 'hands//fan and cup' as they bring her to a point where she is 'animal/inanimate, satiate'. I had a similar reaction to Máighréad Medbh's poem 'Feed' from her collection *Split*, where the narrator says 'I have pointed my nipples in your memory,/like church spires skewering the air.' I loved the matter-of-fact, sensual honesty of both poems.

When I read poems of love, lust and the body, I didn't instantly think, 'I could do that', but I did absorb the fact that women can write frank and sensuous poems about their own experience of sexual love; I recognised brave and beautiful poetry that I identified with. It wasn't, I think, until I fell deeply in love myself that the spark of their tender and raw poems lit a fire under my own work, in both poetry and fiction.

Ireland was a late-blossoming place: in the 1960s and 1970s a young woman poet was more likely to be getting married and starting a family, than weaving flowers in her hair and indulging in free love. She may also have been reading a diet of ancient poetry, mostly written by men. Our society was repressed by both state and church and women's sexuality was ignored, at best. Single mothers were locked in institutions, for example, and contraception was illegal.

Eavan Boland opened up Irish poetry to women's lived experience in the domestic setting, from kitchen to bedroom. By celebrating and giving voice to women's sexual lives, she chipped away at the wall of ignorance and unacknowledgement about something that was real and present. I, for one, am grateful to her – and to Edna O'Brien and others – for their pioneering work. As Boland says in her essay *A Kind of Scar* women's move from being the subjects and objects of Irish poems to being their authors was 'a momentous transit'. I became a teenager in the 1980s so luckily for me the transit was already underway by the time I began to take writing seriously. I sometimes feel there is, even now, a lingering question mark over women who write about sex as they experience it; it's a subject that still has the power to shock and surprise.

Male poets have revered and delighted in women's bodies, but being a woman, inside a woman's body, is complex. We menstruate, we lactate, we give birth. We take in, we give out. The womb is central to our lives and bodies but we never see it, so there is an element of unknowing, even of our own selves. Catherine Bellver wrote: 'The female body is not for woman an external, discrete object, an alienated Other...' The body is observed and felt from the inside out and not the other way around; it is this experience of the flesh which can then be transcribed into poetry, whether as the loved and celebrated, or awkward and uncooperative body of its owner.

There is great freedom, indeed, in talking about the body through poetry, choosing the right words and set-up to explore personal and intimate moments. Metaphor, of course, is always useful in talking about the body and sex – for example, orchids for male body parts, pomegranates for female. (I've used both.) But ambiguity in poetry also reminds me of my frustration at school as yet another teacher attempted to explain yet another impenetrable poem: 'If that's what he *means*, why doesn't he just say that?' was our collective cry in class. There are those, of course, who don't shy from using real words for body parts and/or sex. In her second collection *Gethsemane Day* Dorothy Molloy spoke candidly of pubic hair, breasts and buttocks. And in *Philomena's Revenge* Rita Ann Higgins wrote gleefully of sparking nipples and the full tongue that would make the narrator 'burst forth/pleasure after pleasure/after dark'.

Women *are* different, and it's our very different approach to our bodies, and the sex we have with them, that makes our poetry relevant. Not better, not worse, but good and relevant. In a recent interview about my collection *Tattoo:Tatú*, I was asked – by a male interviewer – whether sexual poetry was the domain in which I found most inspiration as a poet. I found the question surprising. Though he did say that he found my collection broad-ranging, it was the sexual poems that, for him, stood out. (He actually said they 'sprung out'!) In my answer to him I said that a lot of my work is informed by visual art, and women's place in history and in society, and that the body and love are certainly to the forefront as part of that. I also said that for a woman reader it can be really affirming to read poems about sex that are not from a man's point of view.

French writer and feminist Hélène Cixous believes that because feminine sexual pleasure has been downgraded throughout history, women need to reclaim it: 'Write yourself. Your body must be heard,' she urges. I think the woman poet who turns to her own body for inspiration must not fictionalise, mythologize or glamorise, but must speak openly and honestly of all that her body means to her and what she finds there. Not so much as a way of reclaiming the supine, silent woman of older poetry, but as a method of exploring the sometimes solipsistic, sometimes unfriendly relationship women have with their bodies; and, importantly, as a way of celebrating the joy and pain inherent in what it means to be a woman inside a woman's body.

BIBLIOGRAPHY

A Kind of Scar: The Woman Poet in a National Tradition. Eavan Boland, Attic Press, Dublin 1989.

Woman in Irish Legend, Life and Literature. ed. S.F. Gallagher. Colin Smythe, Bucks., 1983.

The Laugh of the Medusa, Hélène Cixous. trans. Keith Cohen and Paula Cohen, Signs 1, no. 4. 1976: 875-93.

Absence and Presence, Spanish Women Poets of the Twenties and Thirties. Catherine Bellver, Anales de la Literatura Española Contemporánea, 2002.

John O'Donnell
(1960-)

Born and grew up in Dublin. His work has been published and broadcast widely. Awards include the *Sunday Tribune*/Hennessy Award, The Ireland Funds Prize and the Irish National Poetry Prize. A barrister, he lives in Dublin.

POETRY COLLECTIONS

Some Other Country. (2002). Co. Cork, Bradshaw Books.
Icarus Sees His Father Fly. (2004, 2006). Dublin, The Dedalus Press.

A Wedding Guest

We stayed just outside Cana, which is actually
a very pretty town, although the military
seemed to be everywhere. The weather on the day
was perfect – I wore my new papyrus shoes –
and the bride looked absolutely radiant
(her dress cost a small fortune). They did choose
to serve the best wine last, after a slight delay
but the customs they have here are different,
as Zach explained. Still, it did seem rather odd
as did that young man (the woman by his side
his mother, I believe) who spoke to the stewards;
so quiet and assured as they fussed over the ewers.
The group with him were whispering about a sign:
a rough lot, they were. But the wine tasted divine.

What They Carried

Sometimes a brimming trunk lugged miles
past smashed-in cabins, empty rills, ditches
clotted with the dead, but mostly
a life bundled in a blanket;
gansies, shawls, a pot and spoon,
a bauble for the baby not yet born

or whatever they stood up in,
darned petticoats and fraying trousers,
a hat jammed on a head teeming
with dreams and busy lice, the typhus
travelling with them to the fever shed
at King Street, the lazy beds of Cabbagetown

dozens buried at a time, their last rite
a shovelful of lime. They braced themselves
against the lurch of ocean and the future
and vowed to keep the faith they'd never lost,
despite all this, in a merciful Almighty
who watched them as they clambered up
through narrow hatches, down on to the dock
to stand shivering, exhausted in new light;

who listened always, they insisted,
to their whispered supplications
that what they carried with them
might be equal to these streets
already greening to new leaf
and what they'd left behind
or thought they had. Clay
under their fingernails. Their grief.

Wilson

Years after all that, we're still out playing,
still together. I'm longer than him now;
now he complains his game is breaking down.
We both know what this means. Ahead, I wait

for him to make up ground between us, and grip
the club the way he showed, my thumb across
the maker's name: *Wilson.* Breathless
when he reaches me, he eyes my hands:

"You're holding on too tight." Is this
his way of saying goodbye or just bustle,
the golfer's artful chatter designed to unsettle?
Either way, it works: up close, where it matters

he's all lobs and flops and lovely pitches, soft hands
that once saved the lives of stricken children
and still have what they call 'the touch'.
I stab and chop, the ball careening past the target

first from one side, then the other while he
rolls his one sweetly up to stop. "Getting nearer"
he consoles. The flag flutters above the cup
but I'm thinking of the other hole, the opened

ground where we'll all finish. His ball
just inches from the drop. Our lives together
a groove worn by my thumb. The *Wil* of Wilson
almost gone; soon all that will be left will be the *son.*

Online, off-key: Can poetry survive the electronic age?

One of the joys of television in the 1970s was the long-running Dad's Army. Set in the fictional English town of Walmington-on-Sea during the Second World War, the series followed the travails of a group of men who set up the town's Home Guard, a local volunteer force who trained to repel any would-be invasions by the Hun. Mercifully they never saw action. The genius of the programme was, of course, the interaction of the various characters from the little town who made up this band of brothers. In command was the wonderfully pompous Captain Mainwaring (the local bank manger). Others included the smooth-talking laconic Sergeant Wilson, the elderly veteran Lance-Corporal Jones (an elderly veteran who continually insisted that foreigners "don't like it up 'em") and the gormless young innocent Private Pike. One of the show's memorable refrains came from the lugubrious Private Frazer, the town undertaker. "We're doomed, I tell ye!" he would gloomily intone at every perceived setback.

The end of poetry is also frequently predicted with equal parts sorrow and relish. At any given time there are numerous wild-eyed (if not exactly teary-eyed) soothsayers willing to pronounce its imminent end. But these prophets of doom rarely if ever come from within the ranks of our own standing army of poets. Indeed the number of volunteers willing to join has never been higher. There may still be no money in poetry but at least there's a little more money for it than in even leaner, meaner times. Grants, bursaries, creative writing courses (is it better to give than to receive?) have helped to some extent to keep within the net some of those who might otherwise have been lost.

But it's the other net that's now being blamed for the imminent demise, not just of poetry, but the printed page in general. The interweb, as Homer Simpson so tellingly calls it, is like one of those glittering shop-windows at Christmas. Pausing momentarily to look, we find ourselves rooted to the spot. Helpless, we gaze for hours, unwilling to leave, delighted and distracted by the click and whirr of more and more bright shiny things. Sometimes it's hard to remember that the old-style corner store has more mystery and promise, more stories to tell. 'Now that my ladder's gone,/ I must lie down where all ladders start/ In the foul rag-and-bone shop of the heart'.

But I can see that dour Scotsman Frazer shaking his head still. Who's going to read these poems, even if they're written? Good question. A survey conducted some years ago suggested that for every three people in Ireland who read a poem, ten people write one. It's true that as the list of alternatives to the printed page grows longer, our attention span grows shorter. Perhaps it's the compressed nature of email and text message that has us saying more and more in less and less. Even our sentences are getting shorter. And shorter. The optimist would hope that the compressed nature of language in poetry may even be easier to digest for a generation raised on a new half–talk code of mysteries. But the immediacy, the easy availability of the multimedia image fuels our impatience, our lust for instant gratification. The spaces in which poetry can flourish seem to become smaller and smaller.

And yet it does. Famously, Auden contended that 'poetry makes nothing happen'. Less famously, however, he proclaimed in the same line that poetry 'survives/ In the valley of its saying'. Hardy perennial that it is, poetry continues to flower in the most unusual and inhospitable of places. Like any decent herb, poetry retains secret medicinal powers: the power to heal and to console, the power to move to rage, and laughter, and tears. Amid the plasma screens and the unfolded laptops, amid the dial-ups and the down-loads, poetry at its best still has the capacity to make a wireless connection between the writer and the reader. A poem is a kind of memory stick, a portable device that saves forever not just words and images and rhythms, but also memories and sensations and emotions.

So why do we poets still do it? Like those doughty volunteers in BBC's Walmington-on-Sea, there may be multiple factors affecting our decision to sign up: vanity, the desire for legacy, the need for affirmation or even just pure boredom. In the end, however, it is not law nor duty makes us write, nor public men nor cheering crowds. The irrepressible urge to bear witness, the 'lonely impulse of delight' is its own reward. Right now, as I write, the screens in other rooms suggest that history is being made; that Barack Obama (surely a name almost in itself a poem) is to become President of the United States. It seems more appropriate than ever to recall the words of Rita Dove, the first African-American to hold the title of Poet Laureate in that country, in her poem O

'Sometimes// a word is found so right it trembles/ at the slightest explanation./ You start out with one thing, end/ up with another, and nothing's/ like it used to be, not even the future.'

Mary O'Donoghue
(1975-)

Born and grew up in Co. Clare. Her poems have appeared widely in Irish and international journals and anthologies, including *The New Irish Poets* (Bloodaxe, 2004). Her short stories have been published in *Agni, Salamander, The Dublin Review, Literary Imagination* and elsewhere. Her awards include the *Sunday Tribune*/Hennessy New Irish Writers' Award and a writer's bursary from Massachusetts Cultural Council. She is an assistant professor of English at Babson College, Massachusetts and she lives in Boston.

POETRY COLLECTIONS

Tulle. (2001). Co. Clare, Salmon Poetry.
Among These Winters. (2007). Dublin, The Dedalus Press.

from Letters to Emily: Finding Your Voice

I love the vast surface of silence,
and it is my chief delight to break it
— Carl Nielsen

a shriek to make Atlantic waves turn tail,
turn a church on tiptoe on its steeple,

a shriek so pure and true it's heard
at the bottom of an Australian well,

as if the London air raid warning
was sounded by a pipistrelle,

as if Venetian glass could scream
and shatter all the people.

Thanksgiving in Florida

The giant roadside orange
might be full of children
packed vesicle-tight together
cheek to small fat cheek.

At a bar reclaimed from the water
a dead ringer for Oliver Reed
blears his details, wipes them clear:
His girlfriend.
        Is coming.
             From Gatwick.

We skim over swamp in a boat
made of tin. Routed birds scarper,
filling the air with a blitz of black paper.
We chunter close to alligators
who test-click their teeth
like just-fitted dentures,
and eyeball the day,
for it's bothering them.

We visit the place where you
were the neighbourhood rascal,
shrugging off the door locks
of your mother's great terror,
running down the way down,
galloping right the way down,
stopping short at the drop
to the Indian River.

Petition

To keep her from Botany Bay
I claimed my young sister's eyes,
her bad-weather markless gaze.

I wanted to write of her trouble
finding eggs, the ones she missed
beneath the hens, those left to glugger,

and how I took the blame sometimes,
the flat of our father's hand on my face
when she spilled or put things astray.

I thought to tell them of the boy
who promised to some day marry her,
"bockety eyes or not," he used to declare.

On disgrace and the need
for a new-fangled envoy

Go little book
And stop disgracing me
There are serious men
And women in my life
And you have given them
The upper hand

Leonard Cohen, 'Go Little Book',
The Book of Longing.

He speculates that the effect of a poem written by a friend
for a beloved contributed to his own 'investment in the
commitment to writing poems.' The documentary camera
ranges round his face, mapping its rueful tilts; the
microphone picks up the tiny dry click in his throat.
When he says this I am ready to nudge and confess to the
stranger next to me in the cinema that it may be I started
this whole carry-on in order to make *him*, Leonard Cohen
that is, fall in love with *me*.

But I don't, of course.

Instead I fix on this idea of writing poems with their
seductive utility in mind; and how it may be a poem that
pleasurably curls someone's toes or smashes their frozen
heart like blow upon blow from that axe of Kafka's. And
I'm beginning to think that a main driver of my writing

has been to make myself smile or shudder or indulge the range of reactions between, and let readers go and find their own ice-breaking equipment. But, of course, writers are doomed to be read and so we give up our own home-spun enjoyments when the book goes Out There.

The time between final proofs and a book's appearance I think of as a supremely happy state, perhaps like what a baby feels like rocked in sea-like suspension before it has to go public. Closer to the book's launch I begin to find myself chafing sweaty palms under the table like a poker player trying to hide her tell. At other times I think of it as the perfect period of jamming, grottiness and the owlish hours and before a rock band breaks the scene. Back when it was just two lads and a guitar and an ancient amp and one of their mothers made them sandwiches to eat in the garage. *I liked it when it was just us, you know, you and me, eh little book?*

And when launch evening arrives you can pick me out as the one doing her best not to be identified as the book's author. This draws on the subtle art of wall-blending and bringing a taller companion for hiding behind. For there it is, in the hands of people, they are walking around with it and their glasses of wine… and suddenly there seems nothing more horrifying.

And among those Serious Men and Women I am, for a long while, prepared to denounce the book as not mine at all. *There was a mix-up at the hospital. As you'll probably see, this one looks nothing like me.*

Which is why the envoy poem ought to make a return. And I mean the true envoy, Ovidian in telling the book what to do (or *not* to do, as per Leonard Cohen's); gently hectoring the reader, be they commoner or emperor, as to what they ought to expect and how they should behave in receipt of these poems. I don't mean the poem that someone decides, after a month of page shuffling, will set the tenor and preoccupations of the book in motion. Rather I mean the poem that addresses and steers and asks and curries and bosses and flirts. Yes, that might make the act of going public a bit more bearable.

Robert Louis Stevenson's gentle setting-out at the beginning of *A Child's Garden of Verses and Underwoods* directs 'Go, little book, and wish to all/ Flowers in the garden and meat in the hall/ A bin of wine, a spice of wit'. It's a pleasant wish for a little book for little readers, drawing in the adult too with promises of wine and wit. Before being ensconced in Kilcolman Castle and writing *The Faerie Queene*, Edmund Spenser's *Eclogues* asked that book 'And, when thou art past jeopardy,/ Come and tell me what was said of me,/ And I will send more after thee.' You have to smile grimly at the man's blend of anxiety and arrogance.

But in imagining a new brand of envoy, perhaps I consider something that combines the bonhomie of Stevenson and Spenser's naked nervousness. In all cases, the envoy poem strikes a particular pose, sometimes craven, sometimes pugnacious, refracting the author's real voice to meet the author's hopes, concerns or downright collywobbles. Next time out I may write this new envoy. It will strive for the chary but charmingly weary attitude of Leonard Cohen's driving instructions for his little book; it will move beyond the serious men and women to apologetically address family members and past loves. It may enumerate the varieties of wine that went into what wit might be found in there. It may well ask for the book to be eaten slowly, the way that properly chewed food is less likely to choke you.

All of this will make for a long poem, which runs counter to the envoy's enterprise in succinctly preparing the reader. But at least I won't be trying to rush the reader into anything:

> Go, little book,
> tell them what they get
> is what they see…

Paul Perry

(1972-)

Born and grew up in Dublin. A graduate of Brown University, Rhode Island, U.S.A., he has been a James Michener Fellow of Creative Writing at The University of Miami and a Cambor Fellow of Poetry at The University of Houston. A recipient of the *Sunday Tribune*/Hennessy New Irish Writer of the Year Award for his short story *The Judge*, which was later collected in *The New Hennessy Book of Irish Fiction*, Perry's first book of poetry *The Drowning of the Saints* was shortlisted for The Rupert and Eithne Strong Award for Best First Collection at the Poetry Now Festival in Dún Laoghaire, Dublin. It was also awarded the Listowel Prize for Poetry. Paul Perry has been a Writer-in-Residence for Co. Longford, Rathlin Island and from 2003-2006 for the University of Ulster, where he is currently a Vice-Chancellor Research Scholar. He also teaches for the MFA Programme in Creative Writing at Kingston University London and since 2004 has been programme director for Aspects Literature Festival in Bangor, Co. Down, Northern Ireland. He is the editor of *The Best of Irish Poetry* 2009.

POETRY COLLECTIONS

The Drowning of the Saints. (2003). Co. Clare, Salmon Poetry.
The Orchid Keeper. (2006). Dublin, The Dedalus Press.

Dawn Sun

if people had smuggled animals
onto the bus I hadn't noticed
the fields were silver in the dawn
churchgoers wrapped themselves in their myths
and out of the earth the old cries came
no one noticed heeded or believed
nor in the road's plaintive appeal

so be it … the dead lined the way
waving farewell or …
hats were doffed smiles no not smiles …
workers stood up from the fields
and watched our passing
some with envy some with regret
the smell of schnapps was something we shared
there were no songs but heavy sleep
pale eyes expelled smoke

and the dawn sun startled us with its cold fire
my words had already banished me
but I hoped our bodies might meet
before the scrap-yard of longing
closed its bloody gates

I was unsure in the new city
tripping over memory's shoelaces
when the light of mid-morning
warmed my feet
and I danced over the river

you were surprised by my voice
calling out to you
on the street
but you should not have been
that is what it had been doing
for a long time
since the time we had met
and before

Visiting Hours

I was driving northwards across the border
into south Down and farther north, driving
through a lean vegetation into summer,
golden and sweet, allowing my mind to wander

to familiar and unfamiliar places. A map
lay on the passenger seat beside me.
I'd reached for it, but was distracted
by the ten white crosses on the embankment

before Newry which made me think
of you and your troubled time: how
you'd hid beneath the bedclothes,
a starched white sheet and old blue blanket,

one which reminded me of our childhood.
'How do I know it's you?' you'd said
from under the dishevelled canopy you had created.
'How do I know you are not just a voice in my head?'

I've tapped you on the back to stir you
from your week-long disturbances, shifting
from sleep to waking dream. You groan
and move and peek out at me from under the covers.

Chocolate bar wrappers and sweet packets
litter the bed-side table. Bottles of water and
juice stand half finished. You sit up, finally,
not with the mock machine gun you fired

the first time I went to visit you.
'It could happen,' you bellowed dispensing
several rounds at the other patients.
This time your one caveat is:

It's worse than *one flew over the cuckoo's nest*.
Said without the grin, but with the doleful
look you carry on occasion, the same no doubt
when you met in Spain two men from the IRA,

two men you say, who followed you there
after three years surveillance to interrogate
and torture you. I had just started to work
on the border when you fell into your troubled

state, filling out funding applications for *peace
and reconciliation*. 'Peace money', is what
they called it, as if such an ambition had a price tag.
I wondered now as I drove across borders

what solicitude it would take to bring you back
to who you were. Not, I imagined, a doctor
who asked me if I thought what you talked
about had happened, had *really* happened. This

is your story, but I know you're not going to tell
it, not again, not with the relish and obsession
you told it while still *in it*. Your time
inside was frightening, but amusing too.

When you were called for dinner once
and I went to leave, you pointed to a bed
and told me I was welcome. The next day
you recounted how the paramilitaries

had administered pain killers. Truth drugs,
you called them. You talked about how
they kept you against your will, how they
tried to drown you. I turn the radio on,

but it serves no distraction and so I drive,
drive on with the thought that this then is the legacy
of the conflict, or one of its legacies.
That after the bombings, the shootings, the warfare

and ceasefires, after peace and reconciliation,
what we, what some of us, are left with
is a man in a hospital bed, afraid for his life.
Drive on. And I do, into unknown territory,

marked with flags, unlike the mind
which is an unmarked maze, past Ballymena,
towards Coleraine, past the bunting
and the painted curb-stones towards

the end of another journey,
the end of another reverie and what I am
left with is the same uneasy satisfaction
I feel when leaving you on those occasions

after visiting hours are over, namely
the questions: what is real, what happened,
what really happened? And dear brother,
part of living, part of the struggle, our struggle,

I suppose, is that no matter how much we think
about it, interrogate our pasts or actions,
no matter how much we beseech you
or each other, we'll never really know.

The Last Falcon and Small Ordinance

No one was there when I returned, not a soul
though each one of the settlers' personal effects remained:
some wrapped in dust, some overgrown with grass.
Axe, file, compass. Scuppet, dice and pipe.

Iron pots rusted. Maps and books were spoiled by rain.
Words sank into the soil never to be heard again:
words like *love and peace*. In this moon-begotten dawn
there was no evidence of a struggle, no sign of violence.

On a tree in Roman letters *CRO* was carved and so I ventured
toward the point of the creek, but again found no sign
of the settlers, nor of the last falcon and small ordinance
I had left them with. The colony was lost; it had disappeared.

The maps of the New World were to be my task, but
there would linger about this place a shadow,
one which no cartographer could draw and the name
Raonoke became the ghost of a name. What then

must have happened remains but a mystery.
Was it a massacre or an assimilation of sorts?
In these my last years, I have often wondered
while making maps of land for Raleigh's tenants in Kylemore.

I have wondered and dreamt, dreamt and wondered.
But nothing, no answer nor salve has come to me,
no visitation of grace either, whether I have prayed or not.
I have lived since then a quiet life. I know my granddaughter

to be the first English child born to the land, a fact
which should make me proud; but it does not.
Instead I'm left with a feeling not unlike guilt,
albeit a guilt tinged with something like awe and regret,

a feeling of being alone under the old world's white skies.
And even if my memory fails me, even if the voices
fade, I can still see ingots at the bottom of the sea
and hedgerows on fire. I see too how history cannot map

whatever losses the heart has held and I hear cries
for help in the forest or rather an echo thereof,
and within the undulations of this wild landscape
I fear it simply to be the wind exclaiming

or my own faltering mind telling me something
it ought not to have forgotten, a clue perhaps to what
may have happened, but the words, whatever words there were,
are still too faint to make out, still too distant to hear.

Ghosts

Each poem is ghosted by another. When I wrote *Dawn Sun* I had been reading the Hungarian poet Sándor Csoóri. I had first discovered his work while visiting my father who was living in Budapest in the 1990s. Csoóri is sometimes described as a folk-surrealist. Born into a peasant family in Zámoly, he studied to become a journalist and his interest in politics has infused his poetry.

In my poem, I recall a journey I made from Budapest to Prague after an argument with my father. I believe, in his old fashioned way, he had called me a 'vagabond.' Afterwards, I travelled to see a friend who was living in Prague. I had been to that city once before, but had to re-trace my steps from memory. Csoóri's associative leaps of the imagination gave me the lead to create a menagerie of pilgrimage and dislocation.

Visiting Hours is a less surrealistic poem. Recounting my brother's illness, I was interested in describing the intersection between the personal and political. The poem tells his story explicitly. In the early 1990s, I had studied under American poet Mark Doty at the University of Houston. I aimed for control when writing about something so personal: to be matter of fact even when your heart is being broken. In the words of Bertolt Brecht, 'And I always thought: the very simplest words / Must be enough. When I say what things are like / Everyone's heart must be torn to shreds. / That you'll go down if you don't stand up for yourself – Surely you see that.'

In each poem I write, I try to surprise myself. I don't know where the poem is going. I don't know what the answers are; sometimes that is simply what the poem finally says. Dramatic monologue gives a writer the ability to assume another identity. After the personal revelations of *Visiting Hours*, I wanted to escape my own circumstances. Strangely enough, some similar themes emerge in *The Last Falcon and Small Ordinance*, even though I was writing about something completely different. The voice of John White came to me after reading about the lost colony of Raonoke. He was an artist and friend of Walter Raleigh who attempted to establish a permanent English settlement in Roanoke, North Carolina. The colony is shrouded in mystery and was either abandoned or disappeared. The final group, which White searches for, vanishes after a period of three years without supplies from England, leading to the continuing mystery known as 'The Lost Colony'. There is a similar sense of uncertainty at the end of *Falcon* and *Visiting Hours*.

These poems are ghosted by other poems. In other words, I don't shirk another writer's influence. I have no anxiety. I welcome it. I absorb what they say. I try to learn from them. For example, while writing these poems, I had been reading Reginald Shepherd, and while writing this short essay I have discovered Reginald has passed away. I knew he was ill and, like many other poets, we had corresponded. I'm saddened by his loss. I loved Reginald's passion for poetry, his respect for poets. He once wrote, 'I write because I would like to live forever.'

The painful irony of his statement is that he died before his poetic ambitions could be realized. He wrote, 'I would like each poem of mine to be as close to perfection as possible, and I think that good poems are much more rare than some believe them to be. I would also like my work to be more than just an accumulation of good poems, difficult as even a single good poem is to achieve. I would like the whole to add up to more than the sum of its parts. Eliot said that this is one test of a major poet (his example was George Herbert): 'a major poet is one the whole of whose work we ought to read, in order fully to appreciate any part of it'. Each individual part illuminates and is illuminated by both every other part and the corpus as a whole. To produce such a body of work is one of my goals as a writer.'

Reginald showed great bravery in the face of illness. His famous blog and his continued poetry postings reminded me how we all face loss, sometimes with regret, bitterness, or resignation, and sometimes with an acceptance that has all of those emotions and more.

So, these are three new poems from my third and forthcoming collection. I try never to write the same poem twice, never to repeat myself. I don't know if I have succeeded, but I'm hoping the collection will be a collection of voices: some of these voices speak from an historical past, some from a present, and others from the future. They are a combination of confession, narrative, lyric, monologue, dream and rhapsody. Other poems explore elisions of consciousness, articulation on the edge of expression and appeal to the senses as a means of understanding: language as a precious and vulnerable vehicle to transport us to incongruous or unacknowledged connections between the disparate mess of our lives. Finally, I want the poems to be, in the words of Jorie Graham, 'a field of action' where a voice's authority is refuted by the possibilities of contending inflexions and intonations and accents from other presences. And then, after all that, I want to make a good poem, a well-made poem, something which will stand up to re-readings and neglect, to being left out in the rain, and to being re-discovered, to withstand the interpretations of others. I want my poems to be something too that my children will be able to pick up years from now, and say to themselves 'he was like that too, was he?' But really, right now, all I'm thinking about is Reginald Shepherd, his beautiful poems, our loss.

Justin Quinn
(1968-)

Born and grew up in Dublin. He studied English and Philosophy at Trinity College. Since 1994, he has lived in Prague where he is Associate Professor at the Charles University, lecturing in American Literature. Also a translator, he is married to a Czech woman, Tereza Límanová, and has two sons. He was a founding member of the Irish poetry magazine *Metre*, which he edited with David Wheatley for ten years. Together with his four published collections of poetry, he has written three books of criticism and has edited *Irish Poetry after Feminism* (Colin Smythe, 2008).

POETRY COLLECTIONS

The 'O'o'a'a' Bird. (1995). Manchester, Carcanet Press.
Privacy. (1999). Manchester, Carcanet Press.
Fuselage. (2002). Co. Meath, The Gallery Press.
Waves and Trees. (2006). Co. Meath, The Gallery Press.

First Spring Days

Out walking with one child in a papoose,
the other by the hand, cool in a hood
and throwing questions and some mild abuse,
we came upon two lovers in the wood.

We slowed to give them time, as we'd reckoned
we couldn't turn. They rose, a little coy,
and as we passed our eyes locked for a second,
on either side of that explosive joy.

The Crease

for Gerald Dawe

What's the river doing now? Does it blaze
with stunning blue and pink? Does it amaze
next to no-one with its smart remarks
on quays for long-gone merchants and their clerks,
on lopsided buses leaning in on it,
or cranes that raise the skyline bit by bit,
on graphics changing colour, shape and font
across an eighteenth century house-front,
on Butt Bridge shuddering from wall to wall,
or the lost ripple on Liberty Hall?

It twists and wanders from the interior.
It takes its time along the valley floor,
so weird a crooked crease from source to mouth
that you could fold all Ireland – north in south,
or south in north – across its fluent band
and use it as a bookmark, flag or brand.

Turn away from the river or jump in
like one young poet crazed with grief and gin
who climbed back out again before the bay;
present it with a gift of swans; or say
that other rivers flow more deeply, strongly, widely;
you're still caught in it, moving idly, idly
on decades-long world tours or evening walks.
You're worked into its endless talks on talks,
the poems, the blagues, the cultural theory,
strange as a Belfast accent in Dún Laoghaire
– Victorian houses, malls from everywhere –
at home in that, native to its air.

On Hearing Irish Spoken in South Dublin

The whole Victorian terrace changes tint
like when clouds go or come, a hint
or Chinese whisper, a catch deep in the lungs.
Thoughts float between the two official tongues
like oysters changing sex with changing seasons
on rocks that steeply shelve into the ocean.
Lift up the shell and sluice one down your throat,
and through the darker months your soul goes fluid.
It spills its love about day after day
of this Atlantic island, sweet and gay.

Baggage reclaim

At baggage reclaim at Dublin airport a year or two ago, I struck up a conversation with a man who was returning to Ireland from Prague. 'Back to work,' he said, meaning, I suppose, after a visit home. 'And yourself?' he asked. 'I'm back to visit family,' I answered. Because the conversation was in Czech, I then had to explain that I was Irish but had lived in Prague for fifteen years. I imagine that such conversations have become increasingly common in Ireland in the last decade and are an index of the larger ways the country has changed.

Because I'm a poet, I occasionally wonder how the changes affect poetry in the country. They certainly don't seem to have fostered any interest in translation (apart the funded activities where Estonian poets translate Scots-Gaelic poets, etc., with English always as the inevitable bridge language). Eiléan Ní Chuilleanáin, who learned Romanian to translate Ileana Mălăncioiu, is a startling exception to the ranks of first and second-rate poets who rustle up their 'versions' from cribs. Moreover, much fine Irish language poetry remains untranslated because of lack of interest or linguistic ability among those same ranks. In short, Ireland shares the same apathy as the rest of the anglophone world about literature beyond the English language. And yet the great anglophone poetic tradition has at crucial moments relied on foreign matter: one thinks of Dryden's engagement with the Aeneid, Pope's with the Iliad, Keats with Ronsard, all the English sonneteers with Petrarch, T.S. Eliot with any number of French and Italian poets.

For geographical and historical reasons, Ireland has remained out of the current of European politics and culture for many centuries, but because of the presence of people like the Czech gentleman in Dublin airport, along with all the Poles, Chinese, Lithuanians and Latvians now working in the country, there is the hope of new engagements and collisions. It is a fundamentally new immigration pattern that can only invigorate the monoculture that has held sway since 1922. There is evidence that the influx is subtly changing Irish attitudes towards Gaelic, with many people now actually trying to learn the language instead of saying how beautiful it is.

Much of this will result in bad poems about hearing Polish or Chinese on O'Connell St, but on further levels it will heighten awareness of the borders of English as a means of expression, inducing gold-leaf shifts of awareness and aspect. This is not to say that Irish poetry will somehow get *better* in the years ahead; rather with the decline of nationalism, both as a political force and as an aesthetic ideology for poetry, language issues – primarily Irish ones, and secondarily European – will perhaps lead towards a new enabling aesthetic ideology. Poets always bridle when they have such things as ideologies attributed to their work, but there's usually not much point in reading what poets write when they're not writing poetry. Including of course these words here.

The other side of the coin is the outward journey, when the Irish poet or writer goes abroad, bringing with him or her a whole lot of baggage. How is one to make sense of the world one encounters out there, through an Irish literary lens? The old way was through a narrative of exile, thus resulting in great ballads like 'Spancil Hill', or more criminally 'The Black Velvet Band'. But as the pundits say, there's been a paradigm shift since. Almost twenty years ago, Peter Fallon and Derek Mahon talked of the way Irish poets *commute* between Ireland and elsewhere. For my own part, I don't commute – I stay put in Prague, where I've settled. One might have the ambition of bringing some new thematic elements to Irish poetry, but that seems a bit naïve: no-one really cares about such far-away countries. Rather, there's a corresponding ambition that the category of "Irish Poetry" itself will go up in a puff of smoke. No decent poet would ever wish to be merely an "Irish" poet (just as he or she wouldn't want to be merely an American or Australian poet). You want to have readers wherever the language is spoken, for it is to language itself that poets belong.

Eileen Sheehan

(1963-)

Born and grew up in Scartaglin, Co Kerry, now living in Killarney. She was the winner of the inaugural Writers' Week Listowel Poetry Slam (2004) and the Brendan Kennelly Poetry Award (2006). She is on the Poetry Ireland Writers-In-Schools Scheme and was employed by County Kerry VEC teaching creative writing at Killarney Technical College. Her anthology publications include *The Kerry Anthology* (ed. Gabriel Fitzmaurice), *The Open Door Book of Poetry* (ed. Niall MacMonagle), *Winter Blessings* by Patricia Scanlan, *Our Shared Japan – An Anthology of Contemporary Irish Poetry*. (eds. Irene De Angelis and Joseph Woods) and *The Echoing Years – An Anthology of Irish and Canadian Poetry* (eds. John Ennis/Randall, Maggs and Stephanie McKenzie). In April 2008 she read at The National American Conference for Irish Studies at St. Ambrose University, Iowa, U.S.A. She is editor of *Rhyme Rag 4* (Arts Office Kilkenny Co Council) and is current Writer-in-Residence with Limerick County Council Arts Office. Her poems will be featured in the Secondary School Curriculum text book, *TY Now* (ed. Niall MacMonagle) to be published in April 2009 by The Celtic Press.

POETRY COLLECTIONS

Song of the Midnight Fox. (2004). Co. Kerry, Doghouse Press.
Down the Sunlit Hall. (2008). Co. Kerry, Doghouse Press.

Where You Are

You lie down in whatever bed
you lie down in, the pillow accepting
the weight of your head, the mattress
receiving your body like a longed-for guest.
You move in your sleep and the sheets
react to your turnings, the blankets adjust,
shaping themselves to your outline. The air
in the room keeps time with your breathing,
accepts being displaced while I circle the walls
of the city you dream. My papers
are worn, frayed at the edges; that picture
I have of myself, clouding-over and spotted
with rain: my face is dissolving before me. The night
holds you in sleep, you are stilled by its comforts;
by the fabrics absorbing the sweat you expel.
My cries go unheeded as I stand at the gate
pleading admittance. There is no one to turn to
as you shed a layer of your skin while you lie there,
dead to the world; my one reliable witness.

What She Sings Of

Once in a time he was the sky clothing me,
the warm earth supporting me,
the all-in-all of every night and day to me.

He was salt waves washing me,
he was wind caressing me, fire igniting me,
the first and last of every cause that moved me.

He was fish that jumped for me,
bird that sang for me, beast that nourished me,
the craving and cure of every need inside of me.

Now he is a bright ship pulling away from me,
white sail gone from me, his rough wake drowning me,
he is shimmer of scales growing out of me;

soon I will sing to him, comb out my hair for him,
draw him back to me, lure him down to me.

Note to the Future

Remember, that was the night we were
old. My winter-fat had lingered on through
June and my grey roots were showing.
I found a new softness to your chin,
just here, where I pressed with my tongue
while my fingers memorised the contours
of where your waist had broadened.
Our eyes were the only unchanged things and
your voice as it whispered how love conducts
itself in waves from skin through skin. Then
the cock crowed morning from the shadow
of your belly and we were never again young
after that night, nor wanted to be.

Closing the book on the open mic

Open mic readings are not a new thing in Ireland. They have long been the mainstay public event of various Writers' Groups around the country. What is new is the steady growth in the number of regular sessions available. Establishing these open mic evenings as an integral part of the Irish poetry events calendar has not been without its difficulties and indeed has not been without its detractors.

In the beginning, we couldn't agree on even the spelling. One saw posters variously advertising "open mic session" and "open mike session". The former is grammatically correct, being an abbreviation of microphone, but does not reflect the desired pronunciation. The latter sounds right but is inaccurate with regard to meaning. Taking our cue from the wider world, we now seem to have reached a consensus on the matter, using "mic" as the spelling but pronouncing it "mike".

The open mic, sometimes deservedly, has gotten bad press. I am reminded of Vona Groarke's description in her essay 'Microphone', 'Usually such events involve a large number of people who wish to read their own poems to an attentive audience, and to leave immediately afterwards so they don't have to hear anyone else's. I've seen organisers have to physically wrench the mic from the fists of rhymesters who want to read 'just four more poems now and the first one's pretty short'. Everyone there usually hopes the audience will nestle a foul-mouthed heckler, or maybe just a crazy guy who'll interrupt the next earnest little poem about Bosnia or the Ice Age with a glimpse of his backside.'

Yes indeed, we have all been at that event! It is true to say that some sessions can have an incendiary element to them with one notable Dublin group having had to move venues on several occasions, at the request of the management. Admittedly, poets have always tended to be a tetchy lot and wherever two or more are gathered, you'll find they've brought their egos with them and tempers may ignite. The eminent Robert Frost, for reasons best known to himself, is reputed to have disrupted an Archibald MacLeish reading by, literally, igniting some waste paper, taking all attention from his rival. Insofar as I am aware, we have not yet had to deploy the fire extinguishers at any reading event in Ireland.

To be fair, it is far too easy to lampoon these events without giving due regard to all the positive elements.

Whatever the spelling, whatever the criticisms, the open mic is taking this country by storm. People are turning out in droves to participate in The Whitehouse readings in Limerick presented by Barney Sheehan and Dominic Taylor; Galway's Over the Edge run by Kevin Higgins and Susan Miller DuMars; The Creative Writers' Network in Belfast run by Mark Madden; Seven Towers' Last Wednesday Series at Cassidy's in Dublin and the aptly named Ó Bhéal series in Cork with Paul Casey. This is to name just some of the regular sessions to have mushroomed around the country in recent times. Even Poetry Ireland is getting in on the act with the recent launch of its own series at Damer Hall in Dublin. It looks as if the open mic is here to stay and fast gaining a respect previously denied it.

As with any new venture, timing is everything. These

sessions emerged at a time when there was an undercurrent of feeling that poetry in Ireland was an elitist pursuit: a closed shop except to those who had appeared in the right journals, won a coveted award, or who could boast a review in *The Irish Times*. While the value of these things should not be disdained, poetry should never be *about* these things only. Poetry should be about the practice of the craft rather than the accolades gained or not gained in the execution of that craft. Celtic Tiger Ireland offered a wide range of high-quality literary journals for both emerging and established poets to submit work to; we'd never had it so good. These magazines flourished due to the dedication and passion of their editors and the availability of funding from bodies such as the Arts Council. They could never have existed on sales figures and subscriptions alone, for poetry is not a big seller in Ireland. Most poetry publishing houses are running on a backlog of up to four years and again their existence is dependent on funding bodies rather than sales revenue. Despite our rich poetic tradition, we have been failing to engage a readership for poetry, with most bookshops refusing to stock poetry titles because poetry does not sell.

Then along came the proliferation of open mic sessions. From their inception, the majority are organised in a professional manner with a featured guest poet as well as volunteers from the audience. Capable MCs set the tone for the evening and ensure the smooth running of events. At their best, open mic sessions are dynamic, eclectic and entertaining. Located in pubs and libraries around the country, they are serving to re-engage poetry with a wider audience: a much-maligned audience who in the main are appreciative and discriminating in their tastes. Thanks to advances in technology, the audience is not limited to those present in the rooms where these events happen; podcasts, MP3 downloads and videos on YouTube mean that poetry is reaching a wider listenership than ever before.

Because of the goodwill and sense of co-operation fostered by the various organisers around the country, Ireland now has a reading circuit, which is there to serve established as well as emerging poets: there is a sense of a poetry community in operation. This spirit of openness and inclusiveness is vital for the survival and development of poetry on our small island.

For poetry will survive all of us who purport to be her champions. She will survive in the halls of academe, the literary journals, the parish journals, the towns and villages. In post-Celtic Tiger Ireland where cuts in funding will, no doubt, see the demise of some journals, literary prizes, festivals and small publishing houses, the open mic session may help ensure her survival in the individual heart and at the heart of our communities.

> Now Ireland has her madness and her weather still,
> For poetry makes nothing happen: it survives
> In the valley of its making where executives
> Would never want to tamper; it flows south
> From ranches of isolation and the busy griefs,
> Raw towns that we believe and die in; it survives,
> A way of happening, a mouth.

from *In Memory of W.B. Yeats*
– W.H. Auden

Peter Sirr

(1960-)

Born in Waterford, grew up there and in Dublin. He is a freelance writer, editor and translator. He was the director of the Irish Writers' Centre from 1991 to 2002, and editor of *Poetry Ireland Review* from 2003 until 2007. He has published seven collections of poems with The Gallery Press. He lives in Dublin with his wife, the poet Enda Wyley, and their daughter Freya. He is a member of Aosdána.

POETRY COLLECTIONS

Marginal Zones. (1984). Co. Meath, The Gallery Press.
Talk, Talk. (1987). Co. Meath, The Gallery Press.
Ways of Falling. (1991). Co. Meath, The Gallery Press.
The Ledger of Fruitful Exchange. (1995). Co. Meath, The Gallery Press.
Bring Everything. (2000). Co. Meath, The Gallery Press.
Selected Poems. (2004). Co. Meath, The Gallery Press,
Wake Forest University Press. (2006).
Nonetheless. (2004). Co. Meath, The Gallery Press.

Clooncunny, evening

Standing outside in the evening quiet
avid for light, for how the trees collect it,
disburse it, how the lower branches shine
with a colour combed out of the lake
and washed with reeds

listening to the sound a place makes
flittings and undersongs stitched into the air,
the creaturely silence, things
shifting and loosening,
a wren now from the eaves

darting to grass, then hesitating back;
standing at the edge of it as if to inhabit
some part of the conversation,
but just the way a hesitation inhabits a language,
no wren codes, deciphered trees

but standing there like nothing at all,
a post brushed by moth-wings,
a stillness rent with little cries,
a body thinned to bone like a hook
the mind might throw its hat on and forget.

'I watch you sleep'

I watch you sleep, adrift in the giant bed
the door open behind you
the blind trembling in the breeze, world
reaching in, touching your small head

the world sits in your lungs and burns you
is a tangle of wires in an urgent room
the world is here and you've caught
more of it than you should

so do you love it   so let it gather
all around you, flow through you
and wash you back
to this narrow space, the nurses harried

cries down the long corridor
we live within a wafer of each other
and have no special claim
but the door shifts behind your head

the traffic deepens   I lift the blind
and the hills come in, the sudden
glitter of the Cash Bingo hall
as the light touches it, all

the motor factors, hardware stores
and sombre houses of Crumlin
gather round you where you lie
quietly in evening sun.

First

First door, first handle, first stair
first zip, first sleep, first chair

and now these eyes that must be yours
staring back at you as you brush your hair

first bird, first cat, first car
when I come home I clear your things

I try to hold on as long as I can
and compose the day from your surprise.

The hat on the chair

I think of poetry as an adventure. There are lots of signs, signals, hints, but no real maps, no sure paths. Poets live in a noisy cave full of tempting sounds; sometimes they might reach out and grab, as onto a handrail, led by a melody, a phrase, a ghost of something. It might lead somewhere; or it might not. After that particular journey the poet will be returned to the cave of possibilities, and might stumble a long time in it, setting out on many half journeys, quarter journeys, journeys of a single line or phrase followed by silence and the cave's cacophonous din, which is also a kind of silence. There is, that is, probably no convincing way to write about poetry in the abstract. No way to write about poetry separate from the mind and practice of the particular poet. Poetry is what poets think with, if they let themselves, and what they see with, also if they let themselves.

I have been reading the Austrian poet Friederike Mayröcker and she describes poetry as 'applied reading'. At the Schule für Dichtung ('Poetry Academy') in Vienna, she recommended to student writers that they read for at least ten hours a day, which is a working recipe that appeals to me. It probably didn't go down too well, but I love her sense of reading as a kind of creative release: for her it's all about attention, a fanatic attentiveness to things; another of her self-descriptions is as an 'Augenmensch', an eye-person, a person for whom the visual world is constantly and irresistibly inscribing itself on her imagination. Her poems, then, are a rapt register of the world and her open-ended, restless techniques an attempt to find a way to mediate that passion. Passion and distance: there's nothing sentimental in the work. She uses her own life dispassionately, in the way a sculptor might use materials to hand, much in the way her long-time partner, the poet Ernst Jandl did, whose own 'Thingsure' might be a motto for a certain approach to the art:

> on a chair
> lies a hat.
> neither
> knows anything
> of the other.
> both
> are
> so thingsure

> *translated by* Michael Hamburger

In the respectful distance between the world of the chair and the world of the hat lies the possibility of poetry. Or I think of some lines from Thomas Clark, whose work makes a virtue of close attention to small things:

> the little decisions
> crossing rough ground
> is it here or there
> I will plant my feet
> small crucial decisions
> they are never taken
> there is only the air
> that I tread upon until
> some levity or gravity
> bears me to earth

> *from* 'Byrony Burn'

I suppose it is always 'the little decisions', 'the small crucial decisions' that count for poetry. A life in poetry is a succession of small crucial decisions, all of which determine the kind of poet you are. All of the poetry I like has adventure and curiosity at its centre and those qualities bring a lot of other things in their wake too: an interest in the possibilities of language, a freshness of perspective that comes out of really seeing things. The poem is only one manifestation – the most wanted and most achieved – of the poetic life. Most of the poetic life – the life of nourishment, of reading, gazing, of not-writing – is unproductive by instrumental standards, but nothing is more important for any kind of artistic production than the continuous life which underlies it.

But to go back to Ernst Jandl's chair, or Friederike Mayröcker's 'effulgence of hair':

this effulgence of hair in the window
hair-effulgence, never seen anything like it
reflection of a tail of blonde hair
in the front window of a car

to go back to the world of material possibilities, is the poet, ideally, a kind of still-life painter? In his foreword to Rutger Kopland's *Memories of the Unknown* (translated by James Brockway) J.M. Coetzee asks exactly this question. He is thinking of Kopland's poem 'I Cavalli di Leonardo' where Kopland imagines Leonardo sketching the complexly beautiful musculature of horses:

All those sketches he left behind –
endless series of repetitions: bunches of muscles, sinews,
knuckles, joints, the entire machinery
of driving-belts and levers with which
a horse moves…

Kopland's Leonardo realises it can't be done, he realises 'how the secret of a horse grew and grew/beneath his pencil.' Kopland, too, is fixed on the world of the material. 'But what does it avail us to be objectivists and materialists,' Coetzee wants to know, 'once we have recognised that there is something in the constitution of the horse, and perhaps of the whole of the natural world, that withholds itself from the scientific gaze?' This is how the poem ends, with the artist discarding the sketches, the poem finding its own moment in this discarding which is a kind of liberation into mystery.

All of these poets' fascination with the material takes place in, is in fact really triggered by the acute realisation of mortality:

> I
> only know this life
> won't be coming my way again, not I
> my heart is grazing
> in mournful pastures

> Friederike Mayröcker 'country rain, july'

All of the hard specifics of Kopland's poetry are reminders of our own transience – but it's the transience of the irreplaceable individual human worlds that is the real cause of grief. Coetzee puts it better:

We bear within us, each of us, a freight of memories of things that have already turned to dust – a squeaky see-saw in a playground somewhere in the province of Drente in the 1930s, a lion on a roundabout with a rusty saddle on its back – memories that will perish forever from the earth unless someone, some one of us, continues to hold them in store. Chief among these are memories of ourselves from the time when we lived as children outside time. Until the day arrives when we are the last person on earth to remember that see-saw, that lion, when there is no one left to share them with save the intimate dead, with whom our truest conversations begin to take place. Death, from this viewpoint, is not then an extinction of the self – that is not important, it happens to each of us – but the extinction of a beloved world.

I think of Kopland's poem 'Johnson Brothers Ltd', which remembers his father, 'in his suits the odours/of teased-out wine and lead,/behind his eyes the incomprehensible world/of a man, gas-fitter, first class...', the poem coming to rest in the porcelain basin 'with its silly pair of lions,/Johnson Brothers Ltd' where past and present are conflated – 'Jesus Christ, father, here come the tears/for now and for then – they flow together/into the lead of the swan-neck pipe' and think as always of the absolute importance of the particular, the poetry in the porcelain and the gas-fitter's class and the tears merging with the water in the swan-neck pipe running out of the tap marked 'cold' in the language of the country where the sink was made. These are the things we remember, these the beloved worlds we lose forever.

Cherry Smyth
(1960 -)

Born in Ballymoney, Co. Antrim and grew up in Portstewart, Co. Down. Poet, short story writer and visual arts critic. She was educated at Trinity College, Dublin and the University of East Anglia. She moved to London in 1982 and was Writer-in-Residence at HMP Bullwood Hall 2001-2002. The collection of prison writing she edited *A Strong Voice in a Small Space* (Cherry Picking Press, 2002) won the Raymond Williams Publishing Prize in 2003. Cherry Smyth was featured in *In the Chair: Interviews with Poets from the North of Ireland* (Salmon Poetry, 2002), edited by John Brown. Her recent work was selected for *Best of Irish Poetry* (Southword Editions, 2008). She is the poetry editor of *Brand Literary Magazine* and teaches creative writing at the University of Greenwich. She also writes for visual art magazines, *Modern Painters*, *Art Monthly*, *Art Review* and *Circa*.

POETRY COLLECTIONS

When the Lights Go Up. (2001). Belfast, Lagan Press.
The Future of Something Delicate. (2005). Huddersfield, Smith/Doorstep.
One Wanted Thing. (2006). Belfast, Lagan Press.

These Parts

It was a howl to start myth, like Demeter without her
daughter, up along the track lined with orange groves.

To walk into it was to walk into the way life is,
the two girls, fists in their mouths, shoulders peaked,
eyes unlearning a secret. It was a fattened, hairy sow
held across a wooden table by seven men. It was hard

to see what they were doing – bleeding or skinning it alive –
some surgery the mountains had a taste for, hands busy
with it, stroking, touching – their words a quiet, loving hymn.
The thyme and the rosemary grew on. To step in
would have been to convulse scenery, speak in gravel.

The track rose into the hills. The woman I was walked on it.
Her throat was closed, her ears seared with death's bellow,
the men's patter. Only then did she reach up to a tree,
                                                    steal her first orange.

A Bottle of Mineral Water

When a green light pushing sun through February
hit her page, she called it moods, talked about hair,
a heat wave, thought it was the thin sticky leaves
of the Chinese gooseberry, taller than us, amazed it grew,
throwing a moving stain. She always looks for the hue
of light, edges framing a metal door jamb.
There's no colour to radiotherapy. It carries energy
so fast it shrivels what it meets, knows how,
like this sunlight, to make a green figure, shone
through the hard glass of a bottle of mineral water,
a leaf of light, falling. Giacometti sacrificed
the whole person to work on the head, till drawing
a glass on the table in front of him was all he wanted.
'The more I take away,' he said, 'the fatter it becomes.'

December Morning, 2007

The lake is running from the wind
caught in an inland tide,
the mountain's opposite.
We cannot walk on it
to get distance, gauge its fill.

Sunlight is playing
a small gold fiddle
on the branches of a tree.
Belinda may not last till Christmas.

Dying is always happening,
holding up its dark mountain
from the depths of a lake,
questioning the summer table
on the winter deck, the unplanted earth.

On the beach, the wind is carving
tiny pinnacles of shell.
Look what the sun is doing
to this miniature world.

Wire-walking and other
methods of escape

I'm looking at a glorious abstract painting where the rhythm of brushstrokes and the energy of colour unmake meaning, do purposeless things together. Then out of the wash of grey a figure appears. Is it a figure? I try to lose sight of it, banish resemblance. But, as Henri Michaux puts it, "man once found is found for ever".[1] My method of reading is so disrupted that the abstract principles I relied on are voided. A human form alters the scale and the intention of the work. No matter how much I've enjoyed the abstraction, it is now lost to narrative. It is a landscape where a human lives, where human things are brought into relationship with me.

This shift in reading rarely happens within one poem. We quickly know whether we are in a narrative or non-narrative form and poets, like painters, are not expected to work on the two concurrently, as if once experimentation is found, there is no going back. Sometimes, however, a breakthrough is merely a roundabout.

Even as we Irish poets work largely in narrative, the desire to achieve the enchantment and wordless vulnerability of abstract painting persists; to remove or submerge the 'I', the shape of a figure, without annihilating the sense of self, that must remain robust, formed against formlessness, to write. As the self is necessarily more present through language, the best we can hope for in approximating the qualities of abstraction is perhaps a kind of abstract figuration, where, as in the work of Francis Bacon or Nicola Tyson, the painting starts with a figure, which is then distended and complicated using abstract methods. Although we can't use words to visualise vertiginous spaciousness, we can invoke it as Yvonne Cullen does, moving from addressing a concrete city 'you' to a more abstract persona:

> You think of a wirewalker
> lodged up here
>
> before foot after soft-shod foot
> over streets of warm kitchens, to that light.
>
> Who'll be passed in the air by the flocks
> of white birds like the best life gets; who'll
>
> know these front minutes of her own life,
> believe in walking rope anywhere. [2]

We are designed to speak, to tell stories and when the listener and we get lost in the telling, the story becomes an art. As Jorie Graham suggests, some poems tell stories about acts, while others seek to be acts in their own right. 'No matter how it might twist to be free, a story is married to time and saved by it. A story always tells about something that happened....While a poem which is an act could be the very last act, couldn't it, every time? It must feel that way, at least – the very last or the very first.' [3] In some cases, a vanishing act, struggling up the cord of language on the page and in the throat, like Colette Bryce describes:

...There
on the stones
the slack weight of a rope
coiled in a crate, a braid
eighteen summers long
and me
I'm long gone,
my one-off trick
unique, unequalled since....[4]

Graham suggests that while narrative poetry is tied to speech, non-narrative work begins in silence, in the failure of language to fully tell. If poets are always already embodied through the word act, then to lose the figure in the field, to attain speechlessness and the wonder of abstraction, we have to use gaps, ellipsis, haltings, fogging, density and fracturing to remove intrusive selfhood and the ordering confinement of the 'I'. These are some of the strategies Padraic Fiacc uses, moving from the resemblance of simile to the abstract inarticulacy of fragments, broken tenses, split verbs:

The dead steal back
Like snails on the draining board

Caught after dark
Out of their shells.

Their very
Outnumbering, swarmy cunning
Betters

My 'cut head' and
Scares me as
Pascal was

At too many stars. [5]

Critic Simon Critchley describes this oscillation between two poles and two aesthetic temptations in the work of Wallace Stevens as 'on the one hand, the imagination seizing hold of reality and on the other, reality resisting the imagination.' [6] This less polarised definition allows silence and speech, flesh and spirit, time and its transcendence, to cross over the threshold and back in either mode. Often reality's resistance to imagination forces us to create new formal structures and restrain the more showy emotive gestures of a narrative subject as Sinéad Morrissey does in 'Pearl' with sentences longer than a poetry page permits. It's as if a poem can barely contain the thinned-to-breaking relationship with a mother and through the attenuated lines themselves the daughter attempts to repair the connection:

> It made the day a room. And you were in it, above another room.
> And then you weren't.
> You saw the room through water. Then from underneath.
> Then as laughter.
> ....Time stretched like falling honey
> and you were everywhere, without a body, watching the ends
> of vision dissolve
> in expanding lines of blood.... [7]

For me, the two modes remain hand in hand but distinct and I aim for more hybridity, importing non-narrative tactics, in each poem itself. My narrative voice, with its acute observation of the material world, enjoys the order of associative images and the resolution that solving a riddle brings. It is the voice I use to tell stories to others, while the non-narrative voice is the one I use to tell stories to myself – I invent the riddle. And yet paradoxically, if the narrative voice is the voice that positions me in 'the family' (whoever is at my kitchen table), the non-narrative voice is the voice that positions me in the world. It's not a removal of the 'I' but a more deeply buried 'I' that somehow becomes more universal. If narrative affirms my relationship to place, people, things, non-narrative negotiates a relationship to emptiness. The former settles, the latter unsettles and settles on a deeper level. I need both. I move between both modes in life, as in poetry. Is it a figure? Or a figment?

NOTES

[1] Henri Michaux: *Spaced, Displaced*. Bloodaxe, 1992.

[2] Yvonne Cullen: *To the Lighthouse from Invitation to the Air*. Italics, 1998.

[3] Jorie Graham: *Some Notes on Silence* from *By Herself: Women Reclaim Poetry*. ed. Molly McQuade, Graywolf Press, 2000.

[4] Colette Bryce: *The Full Indian Rope Trick*. Picador, 2003.

[5] Padraic Fiacc: 'More Terrorists' from *Ruined Pages: Selected Poems*. Blackstaff Press, 1994.

[6] Simon Critchley: *Things Merely Are*. Routledge, 2005.

[7] Sinéad Morrissey: from *Between Here and There*. Carcanet, 2002.

Damian Smyth
(1962-)

Born and grew up in Downpatrick, Co. Down. He holds a Master's degree and a Ph.D. in Philosophy from Queen's University, Belfast. He reviewed theatre in Ireland for *The London Independent* and literature and visual arts for a variety of publications. Damian Smyth edited *All Souls' Night and Other Plays* by Joseph Tomelty (1993), Martin Lynch: *Three Plays* (1996) and John Hewitt: *Two Plays* (2000). His poems have appeared in periodicals and newspapers in Ireland and the UK and he has given readings of his work in Ireland and Britain. A stage play *Soldiers of the Queen*, which followed the fortunes of family members, from the Boer War to the Troubles, played the Belfast Festival at Queen's University in 2002 and was published the following year. He is employed as Literature and Language Arts Officer with the Arts Council of Northern Ireland.

POETRY COLLECTIONS

Downpatrick Races. (2000). Belfast, Lagan Press.
The Down Recorder. (2004). Belfast, Lagan Press.
Market Street. (2009). Belfast, Lagan Press.

The Rescue

for Gail

I

For weeks before (you recounted), he'd been consumed by water,
strangely and for no reason but to live inside it, its sour volume everywhere,

driven to travel under the roof of it: inflated alveoli, cheeks ballooning
like those of cherubs blowing hard on maps from the Middle Ages.

The surface above unravelled and ravelled,
as fulsome and as threadbare as thatch,

the light around below a procession of candles
and shadows of muscle and lungs strange prisoners

of the unnatural aquamarine at the pool bottom.
Cave light, laboratory life, a compelling discipline.

Above, the world stayed elusive, fugitive,
bottle-green; below, where his eyes were fixed,

the clarity stung. It was a kind of rehearsal
but still a mission; a task set; a pilgrimage to and fro

through the body of water full to its own brim
with silence and resistance and serious purpose.

The sides as he reached them were stations completed
by a genuflection on a smooth earth and a push back into suffering.

Was there nothing there below but his own self
dispersed in the silence, his blood everywhere?

There was the mania of his heart thundering in its element.
There was water and urine and disinfectant and chlorine

and still many leagues to travel to where a miracle was waiting.

II

He found him on a paten of silver.
As he told it to you, the silty fog
was suddenly lifted and, settled far down,

a man on his knees was caught in a headlight
as if lowered down on a pallet of sunlight
to the only spot where he would be found.

A man was hung from his joints by the water's hands,
dandled by them, his own hands joined,
the whole of him swaying, grown organic and quiet.

As he told it to you, if that second eel
had not escaped by the skin of its teeth,
he wouldn't have raised his eyes to the lough

or heard 'My God, won't somebody help me'.
A sounding of mystery. Voices of the dead
singing along the coils of the waves,

broken and plaintive and almost missed.
It is a hard thing to swim in fresh water,
harder to kick out towards death itself,

against your will and your better judgement,
deliberately outwards then downwards alone,
away from the shore then inwards to loneliness.

III

A man walked into the lough to be drowned
and another walked after him because it was so.

One fell weeping and alone down the dull steps
of the real water into the cellar of the earth,

another went grimly down, sure-footed, stair by stair
after him, down to the conserving dark.

       A saviour is marked on the outside
by the strength of his hands and on the inside

by the speed of his will and the ease with which
his ancestors people him so he can do no other

than step off the lifeboat, fall on the grenade,
climb out across No Man's Land with a last breath,

bristling, alarmed, devout, towards one man left alive.
Even the failures register with the universe, secretly.

So one fell weeping and alone and another went after him,
descending into hell through the harrowing currents

to the graceful strife of an absolute stranger,
embracing him, delivering him intact and perfect

and, after what seems like years, to astonished descendants
for whom one simple fact inflates like a lung into legend.

IV

There's not a year that he's not visited
by the parents of boys who pulled each other under
or the mother of a girl – strong swimmer, mind –
found pressed like a starfish to the rear window.

There's not a year that he's not consulted
on the nature and consequence of death by water
and all because he'd visited it; sojourned there;
came back. But did not come back alone.

Melancholy Suicide at the Downpatrick Asylum

'On Monday, at twelve o'clock, Dr Clarke JP (coroner), held an inquest in the boardroom of the above institution on the body of a young woman, named Margaret Gordon, about twenty-four years of age, a patient in the Asylum, who committed suicide on the previous evening by drowning herself in a pond of water in the grounds.'

(*Down Recorder*, 31st July 1886)

I

After the drowning, after they had fished the pond with a pole
'having a hook on it', and hauled her out with anklets of weed,
her petticoat sodden, the first lift took her as far as the boiler-room
where distressed staff thought the heat would restore her.

It must have been an unremarkable summer – it was July
but the furnace was burning and the waters still deep,
though clearly the woman, being tall, had gone down
to the waters and lain her body down in them.

'She had taken the deceased inside of the railing
and she just came as far as the little gate with her
when she made a rush back again to the water.'
It had happened so quickly. She had moved so quickly

from the nurse to the pond that no one could reach her,
though the nurse had gone in and strong men behind her.
They worked for hours in the boiler-room on her
but nothing amid kindling, iron piping or panic

was any use to her. As a last resort, they sent to the house
for an electric battery and applied it to her. It is 1886.
It failed. Already the Home Rule Bill had fallen
and militia as usual had run amok in Downpatrick

and someone somewhere was plotting unrest
of an old-fashioned nature – agrarian violence,
gunshots in the grading yard, unpopular and futile.
The inquest recommended the pond be walled in.

II

Surely that pond had lain for years in wait,
the perfect partner for her peculiar want.
Things do not happen. They too discriminate:

the knife in the linen drawer; the open vent
through which a sheet is knotted for a noose;
the bullet in the pistol idly lent.

Things arrange themselves to pay their dues.
So for you, Margaret Gordon, that July
when you knew you had nothing else to lose

but your anger; which weighed so heavily
you had to kneel to rinse your lungs of air.
The waters met your diligence half-way.

And that is how places and objects cohere
with how we move each day from dawn to dawn.
You'd have lived if you'd have lived elsewhere.

But everything is inevitable once it's done.

Interval

In the coffee break, he stole an awl
and drove it so hard through his own chest wall
he died in seconds, in the loo, heart-sore,
while they queued up in the corridor

and rattled the bolt of his cubicle
as the key engaged in a ventricle.
How could one not love a wrist
that pushed so hard and still could twist?

If Anything

If anything, it's a hobby.

It's not a mission, a 'vision', a calling or anointing. Certainly not a profession. Certainly not a job. Certainly not a vocation.

Settle for a hobby. Other people do B&Q and Homebase; get the mower out on bank holidays, the clippers; go off for the day to the shore.

This is stamp-collecting. Getting railway timetables from Manchester in 1957 from off the net, then moving on to the bus connections. Whittling. Crochet. Repairing grandfather clocks in the garage. Going to the shows. A version of surfing.

It's a spare-time thing and with no more weight than that.

If it's 'another life', it's like spending all night fly-fishing then going to work with the wets and the rod in the boot and nothing caught.

It doesn't have a point.

It doesn't 'make life better'. It's most certainly not 'joyful' or 'life-enhancing'. Most times, it makes matters worse; there are things best left unsaid, especially to oneself. That's a fact.

As regards 'storytelling' to others, there may be better ways of doing it – film-making, perhaps, or the few minutes of Thought for the Day on radio. It's hard to say.

Like many hobbies, it has longevity going for it as an activity. It's been around for a while and wanting to do it, or be thought to be doing it, or to do it 'well', or even to do it badly without anyone noticing the door isn't hanging properly or the paintwork's uneven, is entirely understandable among certain types of individual.

Meanwhile, there is work and family and births and burials and time spent doing other things which have value in themselves without a doubt about it.

There is an interesting passage in J L & Barbara Hammond's *The Village Labourer 1760-1832: A Study in the Government of England Before the Reform Bill* (1911):

> Monitor: You read in the lesson *The enamel is disposed in crescent-shaped ridges.* What is the enamel?
> Boy: The hard shining part of the tooth.
> Monitor: What part of our tooth is it?
> Boy: The covering of that part that is out of the jawbone.
> Monitor: What do you mean by *disposed*?
> Boy: Placed.
> Monitor: The root?
> Boy: 'Pono', I place.
> Monitor: What is *crescent-shaped*?
> Boy: Shaped like the moon before it is a half-moon.
> Monitor: Draw a crescent. (Boy draws it on the blackboard.)
> Monitor: What is the root of the word?
> Boy: 'Cresco', I grow.

What is interesting is that one's eye is drawn of course to the commerce of sentences – it cannot be called 'dialogue' – and its educative content. Not simply of its time, or in its time, and whatever amusement is to be gained from that; but also in its use in the context of a socio-economic study many decades later.

And yet of more import, surely, is how that forcing of the focus, that pressure from the language in its shape and behaviour, there, right there, just now, has delivered something terrible into the intimate act of comprehension. Who are they, 'Monitor' and 'Boy'? The anonymity is appalling.

Maybe then there is a certain logic to those lists of names on old arches in Ulster, of people and sites; and especially contemporary monuments, and those temples to the cult of memory rising in Belgium and Israel and Washington and a thousand other places worldwide.

Language itself does violence to us; therefore, we do it to ourselves. Its function, unless deliberately manhandled, and again forcefully bundled into a dark shed and beaten, is to wipe us out.

Only recently has St Dympna's cemetery in Downpatrick where, as the name suggests, asylum inmates were interred without marker, been given civic recognition. A plaque with some representative names inscribed. A small ceremony. There were still scorch marks on the tarmac where Travellers had been burned away some years before. Nonetheless, it was of moment.

The Workhouse cemetery, meanwhile, another two acres of lumpy ground, is at risk of lucrative development on the sly.

I met a man who dove into a lough to save a life. I shook his hand. He need not have done so blamelessly. But he did. He set off. He may have been consumed himself. Why is that? How does that come about? How do those confluences occur? It is one puzzle among many for which there remains no explanation.

There was another man I know who made a point of delivering, each year for many years, to the editor of a regional newspaper, some unusual vegetable – two Swedish turnips, for example, "the largest we have seen this year" and "the largest apple we have seen in any year", weighing 24 oz and 14 inches in circumference.

Good day, Mr Stockdale of Blackcauseway, as large as life in the columns. There is no greater wonder than you. It is 1846. It is a variety of pastime.

David Wheatley
(1970-)

Born in Dublin and educated at Trinity College, Dublin. He edited the student journals *Icarus* and *College Green* and co-edited *Metre* for many years with Justin Quinn. He has been a winner of the Friends Provident National Poetry Competition, a recipient of the Rooney Prize for Irish Literature and the Vincent Buckley Poetry Prize. He teaches at the University of Hull and has written for *The Guardian*, *The Times Literary Supplement* and *The London Review of Books*. He has edited *Stream and Gliding Sun: A Wicklow Anthology* (Wicklow County Council, 1998), *I Am the Crocus:* Poems by Children from County Wicklow (Wicklow County Council, 1998), *James Clarence Mangan, Poems* (Gallery Press, 2003) and *Samuel Beckett, Selected Poems* (Faber and Faber, 2009).

POETRY COLLECTIONS

Thirst. (1997). Co. Meath, The Gallery Press.
Misery Hill. (2000). Co. Meath, The Gallery Press.
Three-Legged Dog. (2002) with Caitríona O'Reilly, Co. Wicklow, Wild Honey Press.
Mocker. (2006). Co. Meath, The Gallery Press.
Architexts. (2007) with Cliff Forshaw, David Kennedy and Christopher Reid (Hull City Council).
Lament for Ali Farka Touré. (2008). Wales, Rack Press.
Drift. (2008) with Cliff Forshaw, David Kennedy, Simon Kerr and Christopher Reid (Hull City Council).

Jack Yeats, *The Barrel Man*

How easy people must be to please
when even brickbats count as applause.

It takes a peace-loving man indeed
to brave such war and not lose his head.

Today's Diogenes must learn
to ride the rapids in his urn

but no Niagara plunge compares
to testing the waters above my ears.

What's a ducking to one fed on
the kind of weather I bang my head on?

I am the dung-heap where the fruit
you plant on me will lodge and sprout,

my rotten-tomatoed two black eyes
the sick-note for my clown's disguise.

The windfalls in this antic zoo
mean not just fruit but the branches too:

I am your tuppenny Christ expected
to salvage his own cross from your deadwood.

If a baying crowd pelts with ardour
an appreciative one just pelts the harder.

Grant me, O Lord, a knockout blow
and over I'll roll and off I'll go.

Catgut

1

One note encountered
the next in a Gortahork bar

a lit hole dug in the evening

its resinous tang, the landlord
playing chess in the corner

and, having nothing better
to do, the reel began
whistling itself to itself.

2

While I watch his elbow stitch the air
to the triplets of 'The Black Mare of Fanad',
the next sound along, just out of hearing,

is the purr of the cat whose gut he sent haring
in search of the tune, its phantom paw
coming down softly, viciously on it.

3

I ask for 'The Cat that Kittled
in Jamesie's Wig' and here
they come now, the kittens:

moving on to my thatch,
digging their claws in and holding
on through the lightest of naps;

droplets of blood sloping
over my lashes and down
my grateful cheeks.

Exit Strategy

rhapsody on a theme of Jean du Chas

Saperlipopette! I trip over
the concierge's mongrel again.
An imbecile of genius
with a lazy eye, it watches me
come as I go and go as I come.
While the lift remains broken
I will be sadly unbearable.

Consider life a series of
connecting rooms between corridors.
In corridor and on landing
I am a yo-yo dangled
from an upstairs broom cupboard
as the chambermaid rearranges
my dust. Perspectives dizzy
and the banister takes my supporting arm.

Always and everywhere
someone is watching and when
she nods off over a *tisane,*
le concierge, c'est moi,
shooing the street urchins off
in between reading your postcards.

M. Machintruc, half-past eight,
don't like that tie.
Addresses and posts
a croque-monsieur to his mouth
at the café bar on the corner
and scans the paper for news
of the Greenland campaign.
It lies in ruins.
And so to work.

The line of a trilby hat
passes the frosted glass
by my head at eye-level.
My life is a broken-
backed *roman policier*
on a two-second time-lag
to the past historic tense,
sleazy yet classical:
Maigret and the Concierge or,
The Dead Man Left
No Forwarding Address.

The postman, rodent-faced
brute, in-out, nine-ten.
The full stops of dust motes
he trails huddle slowly
into a will-less drift of ellipses.

Mme Balai, tripping over
her broom: 'God blows
his nose and woe betide us
when the hanky descends.'

M. Putanesco, nine-twenty,
the weight of the world's
street-walkers' perfume
lagging behind him, loitering
fugitively on the stairs.

Mme Balai, sweeping herself
back onto her feet: 'I remember
my mother as a young girl,
always scraping her knees.'

M. Ningún, travelling
salesman in nothing,
Nine-thirty, an empty
bag full of samples.

You exit therefore you are.
When you exit, I see you.
You are no one before that
and no one then too,
but certified so.

As you slink in past the sleeping
lazy-eyed dog in the evening
the very wallpaper knows
where you've been.

I who am nothing know all.
Madame le concierge stirs
in her sleep and I make myself
scarce up a drain.

The dead Uruguayan
lay in his room a fortnight.
Page after page his manuscripts
proved themselves more than equal
to the parakeet's guano.

Skim-reading as I threw them away
I knew myself in the presence of genius.

River Worship

'Life is an affair of people not of places', said Wallace Stevens, 'but for me life is an affair of places and that is the trouble.'

Derek Mahon spoke of places where a thought might grow, but in this morning's paper I read a cartographer's lament for the disappearance of place, as the maps people use increasingly show only roads, car parks and shopping centres. In *The Drowned Book*, Séan O'Brien mentions someone being arrested for 'looking at a building', an incident he tells me happened in Hull. I can well believe it: when a new shopping centre opened in the city in 2008, an old couple, one of them in a mobility buggy, were prevented from taking photographs inside it, their behaviour constituting a 'security risk'. Public space has become a blind spot, blind even to itself. Where might a thought still grow?

Standing by the banks of the River Hull, contemplating the mud below me, I feel I have an answer. For anyone else, the phrase *nostalgie de la boue* would mean slumming it; for me, it has an almost aspirational air. I exult in, I yearn to fathom the depths, the textures, the tang of these estuarine deposits. Heaney has his bogs, yielding up their hoards of Irish elks and Iron Age human sacrifice victims, and I have my mudbanks, rich in deposits of Asda shopping trolleys and BMXs. Above me hulks the British Extracting Company building, a disused mill. If I were Monet, this colossus on the banks of the Hull would be my

Rouen cathedral. I never pass it without contemplating, awe-struck, its huge, redundant majesty. Fossicking around on Google, curious to see what its disused interior might look like, I happened on an account of someone who'd braved the security fence, the wreckage-strewn interior and what sounded like a hair-raising ladder-climb to reach its roof, from which he then photographed the rising sun, suggesting he'd done all of the above in the dark. I salute him for it. Just under the British Extracting Company building is Wilmington swing bridge, across which the railway line to the coast once ran, in pre-Dr Beeching times. Now it supports a precarious-looking house on stilts, occasionally swivelling laboriously out of the way of passing barge traffic. Across the road on one side is a rank-smelling tannery, on the other a Traveller encampment. Hereabouts too is Barmston Drain, the kind of place whose cameos on local news tend to involve police frog-divers and missing teenagers, but whose resident swan I come to watch nesting every summer. When the cygnets hatch, their mother ferries them to and fro on her back, floating upstream for better foraging in the afternoon, and disappearing altogether by the end of June.

When I first read Montale, to change the subject rather drastically, I was struck by how he had taken a sound palette as honeyed as Italian and made it sound so stridulant and angular: his *'cocci aguzzi di bottiglia'* stuck in my throat like a fragment of glass. Although I have long drawn on Montale, I was overcome with the audacity of Carol Rumens' transplantation of Montale's Liguria to the very landscape I've been describing in the sequence 'Thinking About Montale by the River Hull', from her 2008 collection *Blind Spots*. One difference I think I find between writing about Ireland and Hull is the question of territoriality: I would find it hard to write a poem about Dundalk, for instance, without thinking that Conor O'Callaghan had been there before me, and done it far better. The Irish landscape has been written and overwritten (in both senses of that phrase) so often, and its writers seem to gravitate towards and cling onto their individual patches. In Hull, by contrast, I have never felt the slightest anxiety of influence or territoriality about the fact that these landscapes have inspired such fine writing by Philip Larkin, Douglas Dunn, Peter Didsbury, Sean O'Brien and Caitríona O'Reilly, to name five Hull poets, or the writers I count among my colleagues, of whom Rumens is one. 'Rain is his art', she writes, ghosting Montale in 'Cinque Terre': 'his vocation /to be the storm that sets things flowing, to pour /as the rusting waste-pipes finally /open their mouths and /open their /rusting barbarous mouths and roar /and lather /the rain-fugue over /the staves dislodge or vivify /some shuddering root and pour /his corrosive, solving *stretto* back to the pounding salt-wash' (I quote this passage without any attempt to reproduce its complex indents and intra-linear spacing, for which important element you'll have to buy the book).

Mud is an absorbent element, which is just as well, as I worry – having written about the muddy River Hull and its mills quite a bit now – that I am starting, layer upon layer, to 'overwrite' and sink into myself, me too. Maybe the places we love become blind spots to us in the end, migrating inwards to chosen versions of themselves in our mind's eye, as Ireland has become for me, these days. But I am wading into treacherous waters, or mud banks here. It is 'not the place's fault', Larkin said of unhappiness and, conversely, if place, or this place in particular, holds the secret of non-unhappiness, it is not telling. As gods go, I prefer the non-answering kind, those who reward our human entreaties with the indifference they deserve, in the larger scheme of things. For me too, as for Stevens, life is an affair of places, and this muddy river is my strong brown god. I admire and am endlessly grateful for its total indifference to me, who I am, what I do, and everything else but itself.

Joseph Woods
(1966-)

Born and grew up in Drogheda, Co. Louth. He studied science and also holds an M.A. in Creative Writing from Lancaster University. Widely published, he has read in Russia, India and Japan. He was a winner of the Patrick Kavanagh Award for his first collection *Sailing to Hokkaido* (2001). In 2007 he co-edited with Irene De Angelis *Our Shared Japan – An Anthology of Contemporary Irish Poetry* (The Dedalus Press), which celebrates Irish poetry concerning Japan. Joseph Woods is a poet and the current director of Poetry Ireland.

POETRY COLLECTIONS

Sailing to Hokkaido. (2001). Kent, Worple Press.
Bearings. (2005). Kent, Worple Press.

Chronicles of the City

Who gets to be the last to leave
when a city becomes deserted?

Who gets to hold out over
the silted harbour for a last few years?

When do sewers and municipal
toilets stop stinking and brothels

become bereft even of ghosts?
The fountains all choked with sand

while the last few wander to what
is still called home down the broken

colonnaded way, over the worn
marble streets in the direction

of dust, where touts and thieves
no longer hustle and your drunken

roars echo for no one.
You could bed down anywhere,

even in the public library
with its floor of scrolls and parchment

between avalanched shelves
and chronicles of the city flittering in the wind.

Her Own Drowning

i.m. Laura Salmeri

When I got word of her death,
on the night of San Silvestro,
I wanted to be back among
the back alleyways of Catania,
before near drowning, before her,
my dolphin who once led me to land.

There, in the span of a siesta,
streets empty and spread silent under
the sun as we pass under shutters
down on the day, to hear voices,
the clearing up of a meal,
the fall of cutlery into its tray.

A cry of lovemaking carries in the air
and inevitably, further on, a baby crying.
It's where I lose you and follow
the alley's curve to a square
full of debris, that morning's fruit
market where a few men are hosing

down its substance, small mounds
of the half-rotten and over-ripe
gathered in corners. A perfect lemon
rolls down the pavement, brushes
against my shoe and on into the gutter
to bob away in the wash.

Ragtime

A very late addition the games room,
1910, oak-panelled and smelling of oak.
Sun scattered in to show up white acres
of dust, particles disturbed by us and a sense
of space, emptiness or simply the fact
of the billiard-table long gone missing.
Patrick pottered in the corner, not quite
feigning interest in what the man had to say
as he rabbited on about a piece of parchment
he'd found on the dumb-waiter, then pointed
to the framed photograph of the local Hunt Ball,
early 30s in which among the well scrubbed,
bow-tied and ball-gowned only one was left alive,
the old dowager upstairs, still hale and hearty
while the rest to a soul had absolutely all gone
aloft he sighed, as he cranked up the gramophone
and ragtime roused up the dust, drew a grin
from the pair of us and one imagined, the dead.

Neruda's Homes

Pablo Neruda's dominating presence in Chile is still evident more than 30 years after his death. Cafés are named after him, bookshops often stock Neruda's poetry to the exclusion of all other poets, and all three of his houses are open to the public. They make wonderfully apt museums as Neruda was an inveterate and lifelong collector of virtually everything under the sun. From antiques to bric-à-brac, his collections illuminate his loves, enthusiasms and obsessions, ranging from anything with a nautical theme, to antique maps, Victorian dolls, masks, carvings, to coloured glasses, shells and paintings. The most visited house, 'La Chasona', is in Santiago and is also the headquarters of *Fundación Pablo Neruda*. The name 'La Chasona' refers to the tangled hair of his third wife and muse Matilde Urrutia. A portrait of Matilde by Diego Rivera has a profile of Neruda hidden in her hair. 'La Chasona' is at the foot of Cerro San Cristóbal, a spur of the Andes and near enough to the zoo for Neruda to claim that he could hear the lions' roar. The house, situated on a street of German-style houses, was extended and adapted over the years to end up as three levels running up the hillside. At the highest point is the library, which once contained almost 9000 books and has a reading room which overlooks Santiago. Here Neruda had a floor made that creaked like a ship when it was walked across. Everywhere there is a sense of the sea, from the ship's furniture and cabinets to the living room designed like a lighthouse. Bars on one window have the initials of Neruda and Matilde entwined and lapped by breaking waves.

Two hours north of Santiago, in the port town of Valparaíso, is the least visited of his houses and also the most accessible, as one can wander around without the mandatory 'guided tour'. 'La Sebastiana' is perched high on the appropriately named Bellavista hill, and the four floors of the house have dramatic views over Valparaíso and its bay. Neruda called this house his *casa en el aire* or 'house in the air', and the best views are from his study on the fourth floor. A door here frames a massive picture of Whitman. The carpenter who framed it asked Neruda if the portrait was of his father, and Neruda responded that it was, in a poetic sense. A footstool in the sitting-room is still stained with the green ink that he always wrote in, and on the table are collections of coloured glasses in which he believed both water and wine tasted better when drunk from. This house, too, is full of a sense of the sea, with trunks, chests and ship's furniture, although Neruda claimed he was ultimately an estuary sailor, and while fascinated by the sea he preferred the security of dry land. 'La Sebastiana', in common with all three of his houses, has its own designated bar. Neruda liked to entertain and prepare his favourite cocktail, the 'Coquetelon': equal parts of champagne and cognac with a few drops of Cointreau and orange juice. At his dinners and parties he insisted that serious or intellectual topics should not be discussed.

Further on down the south coast from Valparaíso sits Neruda's most famous house, 'Isla Negra', the subject of many poems and the title of one of his books. For a poet who has become associated with the soul of Chile, it's ironic that Neruda spent very little of his adult life there, due to his other career as a diplomat and a period of political exile (the inspiration for the movie *Il Postino*). However, it was to 'Isla Negra' that he always returned imaginatively and physically for a period of more than thirty years. The house overlooks a thin sandy beach with large rocks and the very blue Pacific. On the day I visited, pelicans in V-formations were flying down the coast. Both Neruda and Matilde rest in a tomb here overlooking the sea with hurricane lamps on their graves. Alongside the characteristic collections of things nautical (ships in bottles, coloured glasses), and a sink in every study for washing his hands before and after working, Neruda placed in the living room a staggering collection of ships' figureheads, mostly female, from the prows of wrecked ships. His own study had two desks, one from his father, a railway worker, and another fashioned from the door of a ship he watched drift in as flotsam to 'Isla Negra'. His suits still hang in a wardrobe here, including the morning suit he wore to receive the Nobel Prize in 1971. He was the second Chilean to win the Nobel Prize – Gabriela Mistral was awarded the prize in 1945, the first Latin-American writer to achieve that distinction. Coincidentally, in 1920, Mistral had been appointed headmistress of Neruda's school in the town of Temuco, where she recognized his fledgling talent while he was still a student. And in a further twist of fate, she was subsequently appointed a diplomat and their paths in this sphere sometimes crossed.

The optimism of winning the prize was short-lived for Neruda and indeed for Chile; he developed cancer, resigned as Ambassador to France and returned to 'Isla Negra' in 1972. On September 11th, 1973, his close friend and left-wing political ally, President Salvador Allende, died in government buildings as the Pinochet-led military coup began. Within a fortnight Neruda was dead, some say of shock brought on by Allende's death. His funeral was the first sign of a protest against the *junta*. After his death, Neruda's houses, in particular those in Santiago and Valparaíso, were ransacked and vandalised by the military. However, the *Fundación Pablo Neruda*, established by his widow Matilde Urrutia, has done a service by restoring all of Neruda's houses and making them available to the public.

Editor's Afterword and Acknowledgements

As editor of this book, I received support and encouragement from many individuals in Ireland and the U.S.A. They provided necessary enthusiasm for the project when the seed of it was first sown. Frequently over the last few years I had conversations with Niall MacMonagle to whom this book is dedicated. We both had ideas with regard to an anthology that would bring to readers and lovers of Irish poetry a new generation of poets. At Listowel Writers' Week 2008, following discussions with poets Pat Boran and John McAuliffe, I decided to start the work.

To include both prose and poetry was an attractive idea to me, one infrequently found in poetry anthologies.

One aspect of my earlier anthology *The White Page/An Bhileog Bhán* that proved of interest to readers, was the inclusion of photographs of poets together with short biographies and bibliographies. The decision to follow this format was made from the onset.

All the material in this book was generously contributed by the twenty-four poets and it is to them I offer my first grateful acknowledgement.

I thank my publisher and director of Salmon Poetry, Jessie Lendennie, for agreeing to publish this book. Her responses to my many calls, emails and queries were dealt with patiently at all times. Siobhán Hutson, the book designer at Salmon, has been a pleasure to work with and her help is gratefully acknowledged. Jim Carney's friendship, support and invaluable help with reading and re-reading the text and with proof-reading deserves special thanks.

Several people gave me information, support, ideas, time, encouragement and books. I am especially grateful to Niall MacMonagle, Eamon Grennan, Professor Patricia Monaghan, Professor Ronald Schuchard, Joe Woods, Geraldine Mitchell, Helen McBreen and Brian McBreen. And special thanks to Professor Patricia Coughlan for kindly contributing a preface to this anthology. Caroline Geraghty became the angel in my house, patiently typing, filing and helping keep order on a project that often threatened to overwhelm me.

The title, *The Watchful Heart*, is taken from Derek Mahon's poem 'Everything Is Going To Be All Right', *Collected Poems*, 1999, The Gallery Press; 'The lines flow from the hand unbidden/ and the hidden source is the watchful heart' and used by kind permission of Derek Mahon and editor Peter Fallon of The Gallery Press, Loughcrew, Oldcastle, Co. Meath.

Professor Ronald Schuchard suggested that the original working sub-title *Twenty-Four Contemporary Irish Poets* be altered to *A New Generation of Irish Poets*. I thank him for this and for his support and interest in my work.

Acknowledgement is made to the poets who gave permission to reprint photographs in this book. Fees for printing poems and essays were waived in all cases in view of royalties from sales of this book being donated to Cancer Care West at University College Hospital, Galway.

Particular thanks to the Irish artist Kevin Cosgrove for his painting *Big Digger* which graces the cover of this book and which has been used in publicity material.

The Director of Poetry Ireland, Joe Woods, and his staff were unfailingly helpful, providing advice and support at all times.

The greatest debt is owed to my husband, Joe McBreen, and other members of my family not already mentioned. I thank them for their patience and support throughout, and their belief in me.

Poets' Acknowledgements

Grateful acknowledgement is made to the poets for poems included in this book. Some poems are published here for the first time. Others have appeared in magazines and journals as follows:

Pat Boran
'Dream of the Sparrow Morning'
Poetry Ireland Review 2009.

'Lets Die'
Best of Irish Poetry eds. Nuala Ní Chonchúir and Paul Perry.

'Three Lines for Leland'
Broadsheet for Leland Bardwell ed. Eibhlin Nic Eochaid.

Mary Branley
'Ruth'
Europa es una dona/Europe is a woman
Anthology ed. Anna Aguilar-Amat, Barcelona, Spain, 2007.

Patrick Chapman
'The Darwin Vampires'
Literary Ways 2: Greece-Ireland Athens, December 2008.
The Raintown Review Summer 2009, Albuquerque, New Mexico, U.S.A.

Kevin Higgins
'Ourselves Again'
The Galway Advertiser June 26th, 2008 and *Best of Irish Poetry 2009* ed. Paul Perry. Southword Editions, November 2008.

'Clear Out'
Crannóg no. 19, November 2008.

Gearóid Mac Lochlainn
'Aistriuchain Eile'
'Translation'
Rakish Paddy Open House Festival, Belfast 2004.
Johnny Doran in Irish/English, Open House Festival Belfast 2004.
A 1000 copies limited edition commission on Traveller musicians.
A multi-media collaboration work between Gearóid Mac Lochlainn and Armagh artist JB Vallely.

Mary Montague
'Festive Flourish'
The Stony Thursday Book, ed. Thomas McCarthy, no. 8, Autumn 2008.

Kate Newmann
'The Wild Cattle of Swona Island, Orkney' was commended in the National Poetry Competition, 2009.

Nuala Ní Chonchúir
'Two Children Are Threatened by a Nightingale'
Forthcoming in *Poetry Ireland Review.*

John O'Donnell
'A Wedding Guest'
Cork Literary Review Vol. 8, 2001.
The Bend Vol. 1, Notre Dame University, 2004.
Poetry On The Dart 2008.

'What They Carried'
Rowan Gillespie – Looking For Orion O'Brien Press, Dublin, 2007.

'Wilson'
The Irish Times 2007.

Mary O'Donoghue
'Thanksgiving in Florida'
The Journal of International Women's Studies Vol. 8.4, May 2007.

Paul Perry
'Dawn Sun'
The Stinging Fly 08, Vol. 2 / Winter 2007-08.

'Visiting Hours'
The Stinging Fly 10, Vol. 2 / Summer 2008.

Damian Smyth
'The Rescue'
The Stinging Fly 09, Vol. 2, Spring 2008.

'Melancholy Suicide at the Downpatrick Asylum'
Poetry Ireland Review 89, 2007.

Joe Woods
'Neruda's Homes'
Poetry Ireland Newsletter July/August 2007.

'Her Own Drowning'
Forthcoming in *Agenda*.

· Notes to the Text

The notes given here explain terms and references well
known in Ireland but not perhaps to non-Irish readers.

Aosdána – This is an affiliation of artists engaged in literature, music
and the visual arts. It was established by the Arts Council in 1981 to
honour those artists whose work has made an outstanding
contribution to the arts in Ireland, and to encourage and assist
members devoting their energies fully to their art.

Cúirt – This Irish word refers to the ancient bardic court of poetry.
The Cúirt International Festival of Literature takes place each year in
late April in Galway city.

HMP – Her Majesty's Prison.

Inis Meáin – This is the middle island of three islands situated off the
coast of County Galway: Inis Mór, Inis Meáin and Inis Óirr
(Inishmore, Inishmaan and Inisheer), called The Aran Islands.

MET – Monkstown Educate Together.

N.U.I. – The National University of Ireland of which there are four
constituent universities: University College, Dublin, University
College, Cork, N.U.I. Galway and N.U.I. Maynooth.

Oireachtas – *Oireachtas na Gaeilge* is an annual celebration of Irish culture,
music and literature. *Duais an Oireachtais* is its major award for poetry.

Patrick Kavanagh Award – This is an award annually given to the author
of what is considered, by a panel of judges, to be the best unpublished
first collection of poetry. It is presented at the Patrick Kavanagh
Literary Festival held in Iniskeen, Co. Monaghan, commemorating the
poet's birthplace and his work.

Poetry Ireland / *Éigse Éireann* – is the national organisation for the
promotion and support of poetry and poets in Ireland. Supported by
the Arts Council of Ireland and the Arts Council of Northern Ireland,
it was founded in 1978 by poet and editor John F. Deane. Poetry

Ireland organises readings nationally by poets both from Ireland and abroad, publishes a bi-monthly newsletter and four issues of *Poetry Ireland Review* annually. Poetry Ireland houses an extensive library of contemporary poetry, as well as the Austin Clarke and John Jordan collections. It also co-ordinates the Writers-in-Schools Scheme, works extensively with international journals and literary festivals and is the Irish partner in the European translation network.

Raidio na Gaeltachta – The national broadcasting station for Gaeltacht (Irish-speaking) areas.

RTÉ – Raidio Telefís Éireann is the national broadcasting company in the Republic of Ireland.

TG4 – Telefís na Gaeilge 4 is a national television service which broadcasts in the Irish language.

The Tyrone Guthrie Centre, Annaghmakerrig – Sir Tyrone Guthrie (1900-1971) was one of the foremost theatre directors of the 20th century. His sister, Mrs. Susan Butler, convinced her brother that he should leave the home of their mother, Norah Power, at Annaghmakerrig to Ireland as a "place of retreat for artists and such like creative creatures." Annaghmakerrig is administered by a Board appointed by the two Arts Councils of Ireland. It welcomes artists of all kinds and is a unique working environment among the drumlins and lakes of County Monaghan in south Ulster.

Index of Poets

Index of Poem Titles

Index of First Lines

Index of Essay Titles

 JOAN MCBREEN is from Sligo. She divides her time between Tuam and Renvyle, Connemara, County Galway. Her poetry collections are: *The Wind Beyond the Wall* (Story Line Press, 1990), *A Walled Garden in Moylough* (Story Line Press and Salmon Poetry, 1995), *Winter in the Eye – New and Selected Poems* (Salmon Poetry, 2003) and *Heather Island* (Salmon Poetry, 2009). She was awarded an MA from University College, Dublin in 1997. Her anthology *The White Page/ An Bhileog Bhán – Twentieth-Century Irish Women Poets* was published by Salmon in 1999 and is in its third reprint. Her poetry is published widely in Ireland and abroad and has been broadcast, anthologised and translated into many languages. Her CD *The Long Light on the Land – Selected Poems*, read to a background of traditional Irish airs and classical music, was produced by Ernest Lyons Productions, Castlebar, County Mayo in 2004. She has given readings and talks in many universities in the USA including Emory, Villanova, De Paul (Chicago), Cleveland, Lenoir Rhynne, N.C. and the University of Missouri-St. Louis.

Together with her ongoing involvement with Irish literary festivals such as the Yeats Summer School, Clifden Arts Week, Listowel Writers' Week and The Cúirt International Festival of Literature, since 2007 Joan McBreen has been Literary Advisor and co-ordinator of the Oliver St. John Gogarty Literary Festival at Renvyle House Hotel, Connemara, Co. Galway.